CONTENTS

Introduction

Child Labour is the forty-sixth volume in the Issues series. The aim of this series is to offer up-to-date information about important issues in our world.

Child Labour examines the issues of child labour, the sexual exploitation of children and child soldiers.

The information comes from a wide variety of sources and includes:
Government reports and statistics
Newspaper reports and features
Magazine articles and surveys
Literature from lobby groups
and charitable organisations.

It is hoped that, as you read about the many aspects of the issues explored in this book, you will critically evaluate the information presented. It is important that you decide whether you are being presented with facts or opinions. Does the writer give a biased or an unbiased report? If an opinion is being expressed, do you agree with the writer?

Child Labour offers a useful starting-point for those who need convenient access to information about the many issues involved. However, it is only a starting-point. At the back of the book is a list of organisations which you may want to contact for further information.

*****

Child labour

Information from Anti-Slavery International

Is all child labour dangerous?

According to estimates by the International Labour Organisation (ILO), there are about 250 million working children between the ages of five and 14 years old in developing countries alone, 120 million are working full-time.

Some types of work make useful, positive contributions to a child's development. Work can help children learn about responsibility and develop particular skills that will benefit both themselves and the rest of society. Often, work is a vital source of income which helps to sustain the child and keep the family together.

However, across the world, millions of children do extremely hazardous work in harmful conditions, putting their health, education, development to adulthood and even their lives at risk.

'State Parties recognise the right of the child to be protected from economic exploitation and from performing any work that is likely to be hazardous or to interfere with the child's education or to be harmful to the child's health or physical, mental, spiritual, moral or social development.'
Article 32, UN Convention on the Rights of the Child, 1989

'Child labour has serious consequences that stay with the individual and with society for far longer than the years of childhood. Young workers not only face dangerous working conditions. They face long-term physical, intellectual and emotional stress. They face an adulthood of unemployment and illiteracy. Few human rights abuses are so widely condemned, yet so widely unnoticed . . .'
Kofi Annan, UN Secretary General, March 1999

Why do children work?

Most children work because their families are poor and their labour is needed for their survival. Employers often exploit children because they are more vulnerable, cheaper to hire than adults and they are less likely to demand higher wages or better working conditions. Some employers falsely argue that children are particularly suited to certain types of work because of their small size and 'nimble fingers'.

For many parents, sending their children to school is not an option. Education is expensive and sometimes the nearest school is too far away. Some parents feel that what their children will learn is irrelevant to the realities of their everyday lives and futures.

As well as being a result of poverty, child labour also perpetuates poverty. Many working children do not have the opportunity to go to school and often grow up to be unskilled adults trapped in poorly paid jobs, who in turn look to their own children to supplement the family's income.

Mohen and Nihal are brothers who have been working on carpet looms since they were four and five years old. They work to help the family meet their basic needs. *'The health hazards caused to us are that our fingers are trimmed and we have to work all day long. Often for a couple of days in a week, we have to work for the whole day and night. Mohen often gets miserable and fatigued with the long hours of work and he tries to escape. Then the master weaver keeps a strict watch on him and never lets him move for three or four days . . .'*
Nihal, aged 13, Pakistan, 1999

What kinds of work do children do?

Across the world, children are involved in a wide range of work. In towns and cities for example, they beg, work in bars or restaurants, or as domestics in other people's homes. In factories they make products such as matches, fireworks or glassware. In brick kilns, children are often forced to work with their families to repay money loaned by their employer. The work is often dangerous and extremely harmful to the child's physical and mental development.

Although we read in the media mainly about children working in factories, the vast majority of children – an estimated 70 per cent – work in agriculture, with or without their families. Here children are at risk from work that is too heavy for young bodies and from chemicals that can damage their health.

Increasingly, children are also bought and sold within and across borders, for begging and for work on construction sites, plantations and in domestic service. The vulnerability of these children is even greater when they arrive in another country. Often they do not have contact with their families and are at the mercy of their employers.

Action against child labour

In June 1999, the ILO adopted the Worst Forms of Child Labour Convention, a new international legal standard which aims to curb the most exploitative working practices. With the potential to reach millions of children throughout the world who work in the most intolerable conditions, it obliges countries to design practical programmes to address this fundamental abuse of human rights.

> 'This ILO Convention must not remain another piece of paper for those millions of children for whom papers have no meaning because their hands are tied down with tools and the chains of servitude . . . Now is the time for people and governments to act on their fine words and good will. It is high time that the world community take a uniform stand and put a final end to the injustice we call child labour.'
>
> Kailash Satyarthi, Chairperson of the Global March Against Child Labour, 1999.

What the children want

- We want recognition of our problems, our initiatives, proposals and our process of organisation.
- We want respect and security for ourselves and the work that we do.
- We want an education system whose methodology and content are adapted to our reality.
- We want to be consulted on all decisions concerning us, at local, national or international level.
- We want the root causes of our situation, primarily poverty, to be addressed and tackled.
- We are against exploitation at work but we are in favour of work with dignity and appropriate hours, so that we have time for education and leisure.

Taken from *The Kundapur Declaration* drawn up at the International Meeting of Working Children, India, November 1996.

- The above information is from Anti-Slavery International. See page 41 for their address details.

Child labour: the situation

Questions and answers

What is child labour?
The definition of child labour varies. The dictionary defines labour as physical or mental work especially of the hard or fatiguing kind. Child labour usually means work that is done by children under the age of 15 (14 in some developing countries) which restricts or damages their physical, emotional, intellectual, social or spiritual growth as children. Sometimes work does not harm children and may even help them to learn new skills or to develop a sense of responsibility. Most people agree that when we speak about child labour we mean labour which is intolerable or harmful to children, work which denies them their right to fully develop, to play or to go to school. The International Labour Organisation estimates that there are 250 million children worldwide, between the ages of 5 and 14 years of age, who are now working – half of them full-time. Child labour presents an issue connected to not only poverty, but also world resource

distribution, world hunger, the status of women, education, economic structure and fertility.

What sorts of jobs do child labourers do?
A child worker may tie knots for carpets, inhaling woollen dust while sitting hunched over in the dark. Another child could work handling molten glass in a factory, or assembling matches and fireworks. Children can be found in mines, polishing gems, or climbing across a garbage dump searching out things to sell. For a poor nation waging a war it seems logical to enlist children. So the children go to fight, sometimes not understanding the dispute and

too small to keep up or carry their weapons. Agriculture also employs many children, using dangerous tools such as machetes to cut and harvest sugar cane. Among the more damaging forms of employment for a child, in particular for girls, would be domestic work. They can go without the support of their families and peers, without education and without time for rest.

Because these girls work out of sight within private households they are extremely vulnerable to physical, mental and sexual abuse. The sex trade presents another instance of severe risk specifically for girls. Real and constant danger stems from customers, pimps, pregnancy, and sexually transmitted diseases.

What causes child labour?
Poverty, and the exploitation of the poor, act as the central root of child labour. Families suffering from poverty often also suffer from ignorance of their rights. Established social and cultural patterns dictate child labour as an inevitable fate for children born to impoverished families. The perception of these children as rightly helping support their families is wrong. A child labourer would aid their family far more through receiving an education, allowing for greater opportunities. Another reason for the employment of children remains their susceptibility to intimidation, their willingness to accept lower wages and to perform monotonous work in inadequate conditions. A child will obey and the risk of the formation of a union or rebellion against an employer is small. Children naturally take note of authority, putting their trust in adults.

Why don't governments just make child labour illegal?
Even in developing nations countless laws and government policies against the exploitation of children exist. The political will to enforce them does not. These governments do not control the globalisation of the economy, nor the need for cost-effective industries to compete with and within western dominated markets. The politicians in

developing countries realise the true horror of child labour. In fact, the United Nations Convention on the Rights of the Child stands as the most ratified convention in the UN's history. 191 nations agreed to recognise the right of children to ' . . . be protected from economic exploitation and performing any work that is likely to be hazardous or to interfere with the child's education, or to be harmful to the child's health or physical, mental, spiritual, moral or social development.' In this same document the leaders also committed themselves to take the actions needed to protect these rights.

What can be done?
No magic word or deed can end the atrocities endured by child labourers. Sadly, it's easy to get overwhelmed by the issue and then proceed to dismiss it. This cannot continue to happen. In papers prepared by UNICEF, for a 1997 International Conference on Child Labour, the authors discussed solutions found in education, social awareness and activism, the removal and rehabilitation of child labourers,

---

A child labourer would aid their family far more through receiving an education, allowing for greater opportunities

---

legislation and proper enforcement of those laws. Once a government makes a proper financial commitment to education that schooling must be compulsory, of quality and relevance, of little or no cost financially for the family and classes on a schedule making them accessible. In 1994 Malawi made primary education free. From one academic year to the next enrolment increased by roughly 50 per cent, more of the new students were female than male. The developing world has the funds to provide free primary education. It's a question of budgeting priorities.

With the children in school their unemployed adult relatives may take their places. These adults could unite to form trade unions and demand both liveable wages and safe, healthy work environments. In India, for example, 55 million children go to work while 50 million capable adults are unemployed. This puts an end to the argument that the economies in developing nations would suffer from a lacking work force.

The more educated a population the more active and critical they become. These educated children could eventually develop responsive and fair governments, to enforce labour legislation and practise sustainable economics. The communities these child workers live in must also receive social programmes such as health care, family planning and nutritional education. Adults must also be taught effective marketable skills.

© Source Unattributable

No cinderella story

Domestic child labour. Understanding the issues

Rights of the child

The notion of special childhood rights derives from the universal recognition that children, by reason of their physical and emotional immaturity, are dependent on their family and community for their well-being. There are a number of international instruments which codify these rights, first and foremost of these is the UN Convention on the Rights of the Child which was adopted in 1989.

While the definition of the 'child' has been a frequent source of debate the Convention states that a child is anyone under the age of 18. We thus understand child domestic servants to be children under the age of 18 who work in households that are not their own and undertake household chores, such as cooking, cleaning, taking care of younger children, and running errands for promise of pay or remuneration.

The Convention clearly outlines the rights and the protections to which every child is entitled. The very nature of domestic child labour is exploitative and stands in direct contravention to this Convention.

For instance, children have the right to be protected from all forms of physical and mental violence, from sexual abuse, and from all forms of exploitation. Child servants are not granted any of these rights.

Children are entitled to an education; to play, rest and leisure, and to freedom of association. Child servants are typically denied these rights also.

One of the guiding principles of the children's Convention is that the 'best interests of the child' should be the primary consideration in all decisions or procedures related to the child. All countries that permit domestic child labour, either explicitly or implicitly, are violating this basic guiding principle by ignoring the best interests of the child in favour of the economic interests of their employer.

Basic labour standards

There are various ways in which employers decide to repay child servants for their services. Whether or not these means of remuneration benefit the child directly is entirely dependent upon the good will of the employer.

Some advocates propose establishing and improving the terms of child domestic employment, arguing that it could be a conceivable step towards ending the exploitation of child domestic servants. They suggest that the preferable situation for any child working as a domestic would be to agree to a written contract with the employer. Unfortunately, this type of agreement is almost non-existent for all domestic workers. The young age of child servants and their consequent dependency upon the employer means that many have no clear understanding of their rights in the workplace. As a result, they are inevitably exploited and not remunerated for the work they do.

In some cases, a verbal contract or agreement may be made with the child or with his/her parents, but the majority of the times these terms are not honoured. Parents often have too little information on the quality

---

In some regions of the world, it is common for children to work in order to pay off a family debt. This is known as debt bondage

---

and quantity of work their children are responsible for and for young child servants, it is too difficult to try to question their payment with the person they depend upon for food and shelter. Ultimately, many child servants never see the money they have been earning.

Alternatively, child servants may earn a regular wage that is sent directly to their parents or relatives. In such cases the money is normally used to educate other, especially male, members of the family or as a contribution to buying food and other necessities.

If an agent delivers a child servant to their future employer, he will expect to be repaid for his services and travel expenses. This repayment is usually deducted from the meagre wage that the child subsequently starts to earn but even when it has been repaid, the child may still never directly receive his or her earnings.

Other employers may withhold a child's wage under the pretext that they are keeping it safe for their dowry or to buy them jewellery. Others will retain money if they feel the child servant has been lazy, or for breakages or what they consider to be bad behaviour. Some child servants are considered to be 'part of the family' by their employers. This often means that the employer feels there is no need to pay the child, as the tasks the child undertakes each day are considered to be repayment to the employer for providing them with a home and meals each day.

In some regions of the world, it is common for children to work in order to pay off a family debt. This is known as debt bondage, a practice which forces children to work purely in order to repay an earlier and ever increasing debt made by their parents or relatives.

In all of these cases, children are being exploited as a cheap, or even free, source of labour. By withholding their wages, employers tie these children to their jobs and weaken them by making them increasingly dependent upon their employer. The majority of employers consider it too risky to directly remunerate a child servant. They feel that it will make the child increasingly independent, argumentative and disobedient, and provide them with the means to run away. Even if they are repaid, through the provision of shelter, food, and clothing, this is only a bare minimum for their survival.

The story of Kalpana is not an uncommon one:

Prior to her present job, Kalpana was a domestic servant in another house in the city of Kathmandu. Although only 9 years of age at the time, she was quite mature and bore the responsibilities of an adult. Her duties in that house included cleaning and sweeping, washing utensils, cooking food and shopping. She was often scolded and beaten by members of her master's family, even for the slightest mistake. As Kalpana grew older, she began to resist the scoldings and beatings. She also started to demand her salary, as she had not ever been paid. A short while ago she was turned out of the house at the age of 9½ years, with only Rs. 3000 for the work she had done over a period of six years. She spent some time on the streets of the city and eventually got the job in her present house. Here she earns Rs. 900 per month.

Long working hours
In Bangladesh, Indonesia, Pakistan and the Philippines, child domestic workers spend on average 15 hours or more working each day, seven days a week, and are generally on-call day and night. In Africa, young children are expected to work at least 14 hours a day.

Live-in child servants are expected to work exceptionally long hours and to perform an ever-expanding list of tasks. Domestic labour can be a 24-hour-a-day job involving a great variety of responsibilities. For instance, the child can be woken up at any point in the night in order to take care of the employer's children or to fetch something for the employer. Despite these frequent interruptions to their short sleep these children are still expected to rise early the next morning and start their long list of chores again.

Child servants spend the majority of their time inside their employer's house, they are prevented from making friends or going to school and are often prevented from visiting their families

---

The daily tasks of a child servant differ according to the employer, but in nearly all cases their responsibilities include cooking and serving three meals a day, washing and ironing clothes, cleaning the house, shopping for food, taking the employer's children to and from school and caring for them at home day and night, feeding and looking after the household pets, and running general errands.

Due to the 24-hour-a-day nature of their job, child servants spend the majority of their time inside their employer's house. Only when they go shopping or take the children to school do they go outside. Employers rarely allow these children to have any free time to play or to socialise with other children and making friends is largely discouraged because employers feel that it distracts them from their proper duties.

Isolation
The child servant is often deliberately isolated. As mentioned above, child servants spend the majority of their time inside their employer's house, they are prevented from making friends or going to school and are often prevented from visiting their families. In addition to this isolation from the outside world, child servants are also often isolated within the home where they work as they are treated differently and viewed as inferior to the family members. This double isolation leaves them highly vulnerable to physical and sexual abuse.

• The above information is an extract from the International Secretariat of the Global March Against Child Labour's web site which can be found at www.globalmarch.org Alternatively, see page 41 for their address details

© Global March Against Child Labour

The invisible girl

The international community has begun addressing child trafficking and the millions of young African girls that are kept in slavelike conditions

A photograph shows a smiling Beninese family proudly showing off their newborn baby to a visiting friend. But it also reveals much more, capturing in a corner the face of a seven-year-old African girl, the family's domestic servant, who sneaked herself into the snapshot. Nobody noticed her at the time, but her tiny act of defiant longing spoke with powerful eloquence to the plight of five million little girls just like herself.

These girls are working as domestic child labour in households far away from their families. Like the girl in the photograph, they are living in the shadows, unnoticed and unloved. Often as young as six, they work for very low pay if anything at all, enduring long hours and harsh treatment, often including physical punishment. Today, the number of working children in Africa is still lower in absolute terms than in other areas such as South-east Asia, where child household labour is also a serious problem. But research suggests that a much larger percentage of children work here than anywhere else in the world.

According to the International Labour Organisation (ILO), 41 per cent of Central and West African children below age 14 are working. That is nearly twice the rate in Asia. Domestic service is the only extensive market for child labour in Africa (although other serious child labour problems do exist, such as the high number of street children). The AIDS epidemic has had a devastating effect on the child labour situation in Africa, leaving many orphans fending for themselves after the death of their parents.

In Benin, one in four girls between the ages of 6 and 14 live away from their parents. Of these girls, only 12 per cent attend school. More than 26 per cent of Benin's households are housing a child under age 15 whose parents are not living in the household.

Children sold as commodities

In the past few years, the international community has begun paying attention. Analysts visiting the region began observing what was going on around them with a critical eye, identifying what is abusive, what the causes are, and what should be done about it. By the second half of the 1990s, these observations led to the recognition that there exists a regional market for child labour, in which children are bought and sold like commodities.

In Benin, one in four girls between the ages of 6 and 14 live away from their parents. Of these girls, only 12 per cent attend school

---

Because migration is so deeply ingrained in West African culture, and migrants have so often in the past been accompanied by children, child trafficking is hardly an emerging issue. Moreover, many West African societies have a long tradition of sending children to live with a relative, where they are expected both to work and to get an education.

But new patterns have developed since the 1970s: patterns of exploitation that are built on custom, but wholly commercial in motive.

Michael Dottridge, Director of Anti-Slavery International, notes the readiness of inter-governmental organisations to launch projects concerning trafficked children in West Africa, but is disappointed by how poorly these same organisations have co-ordinated with each other and with NGOs.

'On occasion, we have noted what appears to be faintly absurd competition between agencies,' Dottridge says. 'It is marvellous that everyone is interested, but it would probably be a better use of resources to appoint a single agency to co-ordinate the various projects concerning child trafficking.'

To start tackling the problem, Dottridge first suggests the need for clear agreement at a sub-regional, or even a pan-African level on the circumstances under which taking children across a border to work should be illegal.

'Virtually every country needs to establish public standards in relation to child labour, notably the employment of child domestics from other countries,' says Dottridge. These should determine, Dottridge contends, 'when it is legitimate to put children to work and what rights must be accorded to young workers, such as a requirement that all families with a young domestic put the child through full-time education'. He also wants stronger legal frameworks. 'There is either a complete lack of law concerning cross-border trafficking of children, or what law does exist is not clear enough for the border police to enforce — if they could be persuaded to do so,' he says. He argues that resources should be allocated to the communities of origin to prevent migration by setting up economic alternatives for the children and their families.

There is already considerable experience in assisting children living and working away from home, notably to child domestics in Haiti and the Philippines. 'What is clear at the moment,' says Dottridge, 'is that it is time to learn from all the experiences which different agencies have had and to apply the lessons to help the children.'

Some in West Africa assume that it must be in the children's best interest to repatriate them and put them through some form of rehabilitation such as a children's home. Others suggest that children may be better off left where they are, but given substantial support, particularly to attend school. This was the suggestion made earlier this year by an NGO in Gabon, which observed that as fast as children from Benin and Togo were repatriated, new youngsters were sent to take their place.

Be realistic

Maurizia Tovo, who works on child labour in Africa as a senior operations officer for the World Bank, agrees with Dottridge and urges a realistic approach to child labour in Africa.

'Child labour is so widespread that it cannot be eliminated in the short term,' Tovo says. 'The families and the countries are so poor that they simply need the children's labour. So what we can do is to make sure that child labour is not harmful to the child.'

Tovo insists that the quality of education must be improved. 'As it is, it is often not useful for the children to go to school, because they do not learn anything,' she says. 'Many schools are without a blackboard, books, or light – and the classes are of 100 children of different ages. Under such circumstances it does often make more sense for the kids to work.'

The World Bank is trying to address the problem through lending to awareness programmes, education, poverty reduction, research, health, family planning, and infrastructure. Until the larger problems of poverty and AIDS are alleviated, millions of little girls like the one in Benin who stuck her head in the photograph will be working as little more than slaves in strangers' homes.

• The above information is an extract from *SPectrum*, produced by the World Bank. See their web site at www.worldbank.org for details.

© *The World Bank*

China's children labour round the clock

One girl has died from exhaustion, but teenagers are kept at work in sweatshops for 16-hour shifts

They call them 'baby-face workers' – young Chinese teenagers crouching over sewing machines in rickety workshops with little or no ventilation. Sometimes the bosses play loud music to keep them awake throughout the night.

The scandal in the main garment district of Wuhan, China's big industrial city on the Yangtze, was exposed in this year's sweltering summer when 17-year-old Liu Li died of heat exhaustion.

She was the oldest of eight girls brought in from local villages to 'learn a trade' in return for food and pocket money.

'The temperature that day was 36C ... a single old electric fan blew hot air around the room,' the newspaper *China Youth* reported.

'Liu Li was responsible for lockstitching ... she had a bad cold that day, but was not allowed to rest as they were short-staffed.

'At 4am the 16-hour shift ended.

By John Gittings in Shanghai

Liu Li stood up from her machine but was too dizzy to climb to the attic to sleep. Suddenly, she blacked out.'

'The gap between rich and poor is now wider than [in] the US. The poorest families are often left with no option but to send their children out to earn money'

She died in hospital that morning: her temperature was 42C. Her mother refused to blame the workshop boss, merely lamenting: 'My child was not blessed with good fortune.'

The local authority has begun cleaning up the 'baby-face workshops' clustered behind the Hanzheng Street market.

A typical workshop occupies a single room, divided into two levels by a makeshift floor.

The upper level, close to the original ceiling, is the girls' dormitory. Food is often left around on the floor, with cockroaches climbing over it.

China told the International Labour Organisation this year that it would 'work together with the international community to eradicate all forms of forced or coercive labour'.

It claims to adhere to international conventions on child labour, and a 19-point set of regulations bans the employment of those under 16.

When a scandal is revealed, the authorities often act quickly, and the press, nowadays more assertive in exposing social evils, publishes horrifying accounts of what it finds.

But out of the limelight widespread abuse continues, sometimes with official collusion. Recently young women workers at the Jingtiao Knitting Company in Shanghai complained that the company, a Sino-Japanese joint venture, had taken away their identification papers and kept back half their wages.

Nearly all of the 300-plus workers were teenagers, and some under age.

Unusually, the official *People's Daily* published an angry comment on its website, asking why there had been no union intervention.

'If there was no union, why wasn't one set up? Is this a result of deliberate collusion by government departments or a dereliction of duty?'

There are no national statistics on child labour and government departments are reluctant to discuss it. International agencies avoid public comment which might upset Beijing.

The ILO runs a 'child labour elimination programme' in neighbouring Mongolia, but not in China.

Experts believe that the largest number of child workers are in the countryside, where many are filling in – with their mothers beside them – for fathers who have gone to find construction work in China's booming towns.

'Children working in the countryside don't see it as a bad thing,' a foreign aid worker said. 'The biggest problem is that they no longer go to school.

As the *China Labour Bulletin* in Hong Kong, which campaigns for workers' rights, points out: 'The gap between rich and poor is now wider than [in] the US. The poorest families are often left with no option but to send their children out to earn money.'

As elsewhere in the developing world, child labour – usually arranged by parents through relatives or local agents – can be a desperate form of escape.

'Sometimes we get so tired that we don't even notice when we prick ourselves with the needle,' a girl in Wuhan said. 'But we realise we are learning a skill, so it is enough just to be given our food.

'Some of the boys from our village – the same age as us – have come to town to pick up rubbish or sell flowers. Compared with them, we don't have a problem.'

Child labour

Information from Human Rights Watch

Introduction

The International Labour Organisation (ILO) has estimated that 250 million children between the ages of five and fourteen work in developing countries – at least 120 million on a full-time basis. Sixty-one per cent of these were in Asia, 32 per cent in Africa, and 7 per cent in Latin America. Most working children in rural areas were found in agriculture; urban children worked in trade and services, with fewer in manufacturing, construction and domestic service.

Conditions of child labour range from that of four-year-olds tied to rug looms to keep them from running away, to seventeen-year-olds helping out on the family farm. In some cases, a child's work can be helpful to him or her and to the family; working and earning can be a positive experience in a child's growing up. This depends largely on the age of the child, the conditions in which the child works, and whether work prevents the child from going to school.

The Children's Rights Division at Human Rights Watch has largely focused its efforts on forced and bonded child labour, which has a devastating impact on children. Children who work long hours, often in dangerous and unhealthy conditions, are exposed to lasting physical and psychological harm. Working at looms, for example, has left children disabled with eye damage, lung disease, stunted growth, and a susceptibility to arthritis as they grow older.

Denied an education and a normal childhood, some are confined and beaten, reduced to slavery. Some are denied freedom of movement – the right to leave the workplace and go home to their families. Some are even abducted and forced to work.

The human rights abuses in these practices are clear and acute. Our objectives in tackling these aspects of the complex and troubling child labour issue include drawing attention to the plight of bonded and forced child labourers, helping to end these appalling practices, and contributing to the debate on the rights dimension of the larger issue of children and work.

Bonded child labour

Bonded labour takes place when a family receives an advance payment (sometimes as little as US $15) to hand a child – boy or girl – over to an employer. In most cases the child cannot work off the debt, nor can the family raise enough money to buy the child back. The workplace is often structured so that 'expenses' and/or 'interest' are deducted from a child's earnings in such amounts that it is almost impossible for a child to repay the debt. In some cases, the labour is generational – that is, a child's grandfather or great-grandfather was promised to an employer many years earlier, with the understanding that each generation would provide the employer with a new worker – often with no pay at all.

Bonded labour, normally debt bondage or peonage, is outlawed by the 1956 UN Supplementary Convention on the Abolition of Slavery, the Slave Trade, and Institutions and Practices Similar to Slavery.

Millions of children work as bonded child labourers in countries around the world, 15 million in India alone; the full extent of the problem has yet to be shown. Many are subjected to severe physical abuse, as in a case cited in the July 1995 Human Rights Watch report, *Contemporary Forms of Slavery in Pakistan.*

'Two years ago at the age of seven, Anwar started weaving carpets in a village in Pakistan's province of Sindh. He was given some food, little free time, and no medical assistance. He was told repeatedly that he could not stop working until he earned enough money to pay an alleged family debt. He was never told who in his family had borrowed money nor how much he had borrowed. Any time he made an error with his work, he was fined and the debt increased. Once when his work was considered to be too slow, he was beaten with a stick. Once after a particularly painful beating, he tried to run away, only to be apprehended by the local police who forcibly returned him to the carpet looms.'

On the advocacy front, we have met with children's and human rights groups, as well as representatives from the United Nations Children's Fund (UNICEF), the International Labour Organisation (ILO), the World Bank, and other organisations, to try to develop a holistic strategy to prevent children from losing their childhood, education, and opportunities by being entrapped in bonded labour.

We have also worked to provide to children's organisations and international advocacy groups objective on-the-spot reporting to support efforts to effect change.

• The above information is an extract from Human Rights Watch's web site which can be found at www.hrw.org Alternatively see page 41 for their postal address details.

© 2001, *Human Rights Watch*

Worst forms of child labour

Global data

Total child labour
World-wide statistics
• Of the estimated 250 million children between the ages of 5 and 14 who are economically active, some 50 million to 60 million between the ages of 5 and 11 are engaged in such intolerable forms of labour.
(*The Progress of Nations* 2000 © The United Nations Children's Fund (UNICEF), New York, 2000)
• The ILO estimated that 250 million children between 5 and 14 worked for a living, and that over 50 million children under age twelve worked in hazardous circumstances.
(ILO, *Child Labour, Targeting the Intolerable*, ILO Geneva, November 1996)

General notes and observations
• Around the world, children face dangerous and unhealthy conditions, working in factories, fields, and sweatshops, as domestic servants, or, in some cases, as prostitutes. The trafficking of children for forced labour, prostitution, and pornography is a growing and lucrative business for criminals. In many cities large numbers of street children lack shelter, food, education, and support and are vulnerable to many forms of abuse, despite the best efforts of governments and NGOs. In countries such as Colombia, Sri Lanka, Sierra Leone, and Uganda, armed rebels force children to serve as soldiers or recruit them with promises or threats.
(US Dept of State, *Human Rights Report*, 2001)

Child trafficking
World-wide statistics
• Trafficking in persons is a fundamental and crucially important challenge in the areas of human rights and law enforcement. Based on reliable estimates, at least 700,000 persons to 2 million, especially women and children, are trafficked each year across international borders. Victims are forced to toil in sweatshops, construction sites, brothels, and fields. Deprived of the most fundamental human rights, subjected to threats and violence, victims of trafficking are made to toil under horrific conditions in sweatshops and on construction sites, in fields and in brothels. Women and children, some as young as seven years old, are forced to labour in sex industries where they suffer physical and mental abuse and are exposed to disease, including infection by the HIV virus.
(US Dept of State, *Trafficking in Persons Report*, 12 July 2001 citing Secretary Powell and others, Remarks at Special Briefing Washington, DC, 12 July 2001).

Child prostitution
General notes and observations
• Each year, some one million children enter the sex trade, exploited by people or circum-

stances. Because of the criminal nature of commercial sexual exploitation of children, it is difficult to collect accurate data. However, it is known to be a multi-billion-dollar sex trade, into which each year some one million children are drawn. Research suggests that the age of the children involved is decreasing. Most are poor children between the ages of 13 and 18, although there is evidence that very young children, babies even, are also caught up in this horrific trade. They come from all parts of the world.

(World Congress Against Commercial Sexual Exploitation of Children, 27-31 August 1996)

Child slavery
Adult statistics
- 1999 United Nations estimate that there were 20 million bonded labourers world-wide.
  (ICFTU/Anti Slavery, *Forced labour in the 21st century*, Dec 2001, citing UN working group on contemporary forms of slavery)

Children in crime – child soldiers
World-wide statistics
- The Coalition to Stop the Use of Child Soldiers estimated that approximately 300,000 children under the age of eighteen fought in armed conflicts world-wide.
  (CSUCS, *Global Report on Child Soldiers – 2001*, 12 June 2001)
- The problem is most critical in Africa and Asia, though children are used as soldiers by governments and armed groups in many countries in the Americas, Europe and Middle East.
  (CSUCS, *Global Report on Child Soldiers*)
- In many countries, both girls and boys are used as soldiers; girls are at particular risk of rape, sexual harassment and abuse.
  (CSUCS, *Global Report on Child Soldiers*)
- At any one time, more than 300,000 children under 18 – girls and boys – are fighting as soldiers with government armed forces and armed opposition groups in more than 30 countries world-

wide. In more than 85 countries, hundreds of thousands more under-18s have been recruited into government armed forces, paramilitaries, civil militia and a wide variety of non-state armed groups. Millions of children world-wide receive military training and indoctrination in youth movements and schools. While most child soldiers are aged between 15 and 18, the youngest age recorded in this report is seven.

(CSUCS, *Global Report on Child Soldiers – 2001*, 12 June 2001)

Domestic child servants
World-wide statistics
- The ILO estimated that 250 million children between 5 and 14 worked for a living, and that over 50 million children under age twelve worked in hazardous circumstances. It also estimates that domestic work is the largest employment category of girls under age 16 in the world.
  (ILO, *Child Labour, Targeting the Intolerable*, ILO Geneva, November 1996)

General notes and observations
- The majority of child domestic workers tend to be between 12 and 17 years old, but some surveys

have identified children as young as 5 or 6 years old.
  (ILO *Calls for Immediate Action Against Intolerable Forms of Child Labour*, 12 November 1996)
- Hundreds of thousands of girls, approximately 10 per cent of the child labour force, work long days as domestic workers in an environment where beatings, insults and sexual harassment are all too common.
  (ILO, *The Most Intolerable Forms of Child Labour Targeted at the Cartagena Meeting*, 7 May 1997)

Other hazardous child labour
World-wide statistics
- The ILO estimated that 250 million children between 5 and 14 worked for a living, and that over 50 million children under age twelve worked in hazardous circumstances. It also estimates that domestic work is the largest employment category of girls under age 16 in the world.
  (ILO *Child Labour, Targeting the Intolerable*, ILO Geneva, November 1996)

- The above information is an extract from the International Secretariat of the Global March Against Child Labour's web site which can be found at www.globalmarch.org
  © *Global March Against Child Labour*

Child workers

Working rates among 10- 14-year-old children around the world

Kenya	41.3%
Senegal	31.4%
Bangladesh	30.1%
Nigeria	25.8%
Turkey	24%
Côte d'Ivoire	20.5%
Pakistan	17.7%
Brazil	16.1%
India	14.4%
China	11.6%
Egypt	11.2%
Mexico	6.7%
Argentina	4.5%
Portugal	1.8%
Italy	0.4%

World Socialist web site, Dipak Basu, Child Labour and Child Slaves, 7 January 2000

Slave trade or fair trade?

How can you identify which products use slave labour or guarantee an item is 'slave free'? Contrary to popular belief, few goods for sale in the West have been made using slave labour, but it can and does happen.

Determining whether slavery or another form of exploited labour has been used is difficult. The supply chains involved are often complex and, in sectors such as the garment industry, companies may employ suppliers who in turn may employ many subcontractors. Clearly, this makes it difficult to source a product's ingredients. It is often easier to identify which products have not been tainted by slavery than those that have.

But despite the difficulties, there are ways consumers can buy goods which they can be confident have been produced without slavery. The two main methods are by purchasing fairly traded goods or products made by companies that are members of an ethical trade association.

Fair trade production guarantees that no forced labour or illegal child labour has been used at any stage, including labour used by producers and importers. In order to encourage mainstream companies to participate in fair trade, a labelling system has been developed which is operating in 17 countries. In the UK there is the Fairtrade Mark, in Holland and France fair trade products carry the Max Havelaar label and in Germany there is Transfair. All are co-ordinated by Fairtrade Labelling Organisations International based in Germany.

As well as being a guarantee that no slave labour has been used, fair trade products ensure producers receive a fair price for their produce, providing an alternative to the unfair trading systems that keep people in poverty and can force them into slavery. But one of the problems with this system is it only applies to a small number of producers.

Ethical trade attempts to encourage companies to improve employment conditions at every stage in the supply chain for products

anti-slavery
today's fight for tomorrow's freedom

destined for the Western market. Developed through such organisations as the Ethical Trading Initiative in Britain (Anti-Slavery is a member of the ETI), and the Fair Labor Association and SA8000 in the US, ethical trade's approach is distinguished by the equal participation of trade unions, companies and non-governmental organisations. Together they agree a code of minimum labour standards and develop systems to monitor as well as verify its implementation.

These standards reflect the International Labour Organisation's core principles prohibiting forced labour, illegal child labour, harsh or inhumane treatment, discrimination, and call for freedom of association, minimum wage, health and safety, reasonable hours of work and overtime pay.

Participating companies agree to adopt these standards and to work with their suppliers to ensure they do the same. If it is not possible to apply all of these principles immediately, a time frame for transition is drawn up. Serious breaches of standards, such as those of forced labour and inhumane treatment, must be corrected immediately otherwise membership of the association is ended. Members initially determine compliance through a company audit, which is followed by a regular and ongoing monitoring and verification process.

Many companies have sought to counter criticisms by drawing up their own codes of conduct. However, these codes vary greatly, as does their implementation. Trade unions and non-governmental organisations are concerned that such codes are problematic when written unilaterally and implemented by companies, as they exclude workers from negotiations over their employment conditions. Often these codes may omit core labour standards, particularly with regard to child labour and freedom of association. They also lack independent monitoring and verification. In many cases inspections are announced so when monitors visit there is no evidence of a breach of standards. Frequently the monitors used are inexperienced, poorly trained and too willing to accept statements made by management. Even more seriously, workers may be threatened to overstate their wages and understate their working hours when questioned.

Because the principle of ethical trade is relatively new it is evolving and faces obstacles and challenges to its implementation. It is essential that companies are encouraged to join initiatives, such as the ETI, that guarantee independent monitoring and verification of labour standards and provide a framework for companies to develop common principles for implementation.

While not in itself an end to the problem of forced and illegal child labour, in some industries it is one strategy that can be used to hold companies to account.

● Further information and copies of Anti-Slavery's new campaign are available to download from their web site at www.antislavery.org To find out which companies are participating in ethical trade, visit www.eti.org, www.fairlabor.org and www.cepaa.org

● The above information is an extract from *Reporter*, the publication produced by Anti-Slavery International. See page 41 for their address details.

© Anti-Slavery International

The bitter taste of chocolate

Child labour in Côte d'Ivoire and Ghana

Chocolate companies in the West are finally starting to wake up to the reality that child labour is being used on the cocoa plantations that supply the companies with the raw material to make their chocolate. Some key players in the US and Britain are starting to make noise on the issue, although they have a long way to go.

The US Chocolate Manufacturers' Association (CMA) has pledged to help fight child labour in Côte d'Ivoire and Ghana, countries that are the world's leading producers of cocoa.

Owners and managers of the countries' expansive cocoa plantations use children to clear land for the planting of cocoa trees, weed the plantations, harvest the crops, and perform other duties. The children are unpaid or paid pitiful amounts. Côte d'Ivoire is the world's largest producer of cocoa, accounting for 40 per cent of the world output, while Ghana ranks second. Extracts from cocoa are used in the beverage industry and also to make chocolate.

CMA intends to come up with an action plan that will build upon the results of a study of some 3,000 farms in Côte d'Ivoire and Ghana. The CMA, which brings together some of the leading chocolate manufacturers such as Hershey, Nestlé USA, and M&M Mars, has stated that it will collaborate with other trade associations and the two governments to find ways to eradicate this exploitation of children.

The move by CMA came a few weeks after chocolate companies in Britain vowed that they would enact measures to curb the use of child labourers in the plantations. The companies were reacting to a Channel 4 documentary that reported that most of the cocoa imported into the country was produced using child labour, especially in Côte d'Ivoire.

With cocoa being the one of the largest foreign exchange earners

By Matthias Muindi, AFRICANEWS

for the two countries, high-level delegations immediately left Abidjan and Accra for London in the middle of June to 'present the actual picture' after Côte d'Ivoire's ambassador to the UK, Kouadio Adjoumani, called the documentary 'nonsense' and 'wildly inaccurate'. 'The absurdity of the claim that 90 per cent of farms use slave labour is shown up by the simple fact that this would mean that nearly every one of the 700,000 farmers employs slaves, patently nonsense as anyone with any knowledge of our country would know,' he had said.

> **In the face of low prices, most of the cocoa farmers have resorted to using cheap labour, which is a breeding ground for slavery**

But much as the delegations tried to use softer language to deal with the British Foreign Office, they agreed with the ambassador's sentiments. The Ivorian delegation defended the cocoa farmers by accusing the chocolate multinationals of deliberately keeping cocoa prices low, consequently consigning the farmers to live in poverty.

In the face of low prices, most of the cocoa farmers have resorted to using cheap labour, which is a breeding ground for slavery. Therefore, if slavery is to be eradicated, said Côte d'Ivoire Prime Minister Pascal N'Guessan, then the chocolate giants must pay more to the farmers. This, he said, will ensure quality of life for the seven million Ivorians who depend on cocoa farming and also discourage poorer families from selling their children to traffickers.

At the end of the meeting, the British Foreign Office minister Brian Wilson promised to set up a task force to investigate the use of child labourers. Wilson, who had also indicated that he would meet later with chocolate executives to persuade them to offer a better price, ruled out a boycott of the cocoa imports claiming such a measure would deepen 'the poverty on which slavery thrives'.

World cocoa prices are at a 10-year low, with some farmers having been forced to burn small amounts of the crop to boost the prices. The low prices are blamed on over-production and middlemen who have invaded the now deregulated cocoa market. These brokers prohibit small farmers from dealing directly with the large firms, which takes away the farmers' bargaining power. The brokers also do not disclose the source of their cocoa, making it hard to identify cocoa that was produced using child labour.

With the spotlight having been cast on the industry, international cocoa traders and manufacturers were quick to say that the documentary was exaggerated. 'We do not believe that the farms visited by the pro-gramme are in the least representa-tive of cocoa farming in Côte d'Ivoire, although the claims cannot be ignored,' said the Biscuit, Cake, Chocolate, and Confectionery Alliance (BCCCA). BCCCA denied fixing prices and instead blamed the low prices on the 'laws of supply and demand'. 'We have relatively high production, relatively high stocks and fairly static demand. Unfortunately that is not a recipe for high prices,' said John Newman, BCCCA's spokesman.

But even with this chest thump-ing, the industry was on the defen-sive. Cadbury, which imports 90 per cent of its cocoa from Ghana, quickly promised to fight the use of child labour in the cocoa plantations. 'What we need to do is to support the efforts of those African govern-ments which are trying to tackle this,' said company spokesman Richard Frost. He was quick to add that such a campaign needs to be done on a worldwide level since the use of child labour is not confined to the chocolate industry alone.

None of these chocolate giants, however, have announced concrete plans on how they will deal with the issue of child labour, nor have they pledged to expose offenders in the industry. There are also no indica-tions that these conglomerates will offer better prices. Also unsettling is silence by Western countries, which are the largest consumers of chocolate.

So far, the only country that has set aside funds to deal with the issue is Japan, which last month announced that it would donate US$980,000 to Benin to support efforts to reduce poverty and combat child trafficking in Benin.

It was from Benin that the ugly face of child slavery reared its head in April, when a Nigerian registered ship, Mv *Etinero*, was impounded while trafficking child slaves from different countries in the sub-region.

Early this month, Benin's National Assembly ratified the 1998 International Labour Organisation (ILO) Convention 182 that prohibits the worst forms of child labour and the 1990 UN Convention on the Rights of the Child. At the same time in Mali, the country's parliament approved a law that would make child trafficking punishable by five to 20 years in prison. Mali took such an action as it is currently short of funds to repatriate, rehabilitate and resettle 15,000 Mali child slaves currently working in Côte d'Ivoire in conditions that have been described as akin to hell. Nigeria recently passed a similar bill that aims to deal with human traffickers.

Noble as such efforts are, monitoring the use of child workers is both an expansive and expensive exercise. This is due to a shortage of personnel and resources to track down perpetrators, and the complicated nature of legitimate business operations in the concerned countries. For example, the entrance of middlemen in the cocoa industry who are only interested in the crop means that they will look the other way as long as production goes on.

On April 17, Red Cross societies in sixteen West African nations announced that they would set up teams to monitor the region's main ports and track down traffickers. But it is not easy to monitor the West African coastline, as there is no international naval presence in the area. The British Royal Navy used to have a ship in the area until the 1990s, but withdrew it because of budget cuts.

So the war to fight a menace that was criminalised by the UN General Assembly in 1994 is far from being won. According to a report commissioned by UNICEF last year, about 200,000 children are trafficked each year in the West and Central Africa sub-region alone, with minors being purchased for as little as US$10 from Benin, Togo, Mali, Niger and Nigeria. They are then shipped to work with no pay in homes, cocoa and coffee plantations, fishing boats and mines in Cameroon, Gabon, Côte d'Ivoire, The Gambia and Equatorial Guinea. Some from Nigeria are even purchased to work as sex slaves.

The children are vulnerable because of poverty and wars that have disrupted people's lives in the past decade. Analysts also agree that the opening up of common borders by the regional trade body, ECOWAS, to promote free trade has also contributed to the prob-lem, since it makes it difficult to distinguish between criminal trafficking and cross-border migration. UNICEF, the World Bank, and ILO agree that poverty is the largest causal factor in the shipment of children.

Data by the three institutions estimate that 40 per cent of the population in West Africa lives below the poverty line, with the level in some countries being as high as 72 per cent. 'In the past few years, because of the deteriorating eco-nomic situation, there has been a much bigger trade in children . . . particularly large plantations which need a lot of cheap labour, obedient labour and children are perfect for that,' says Esther Guluma, a UNICEF official in Benin. And with most of the governments possessing in-adequate legislation against child trafficking and labour, the perpetrators have a field day.

'Chocolate slaves' carry many scars

British children love chocolate. Each year they spend £1.2 billion of their pocket money to buy it, about a third of the total amount spent nationally on the product. Britons ate 550,000 tons last year, again a third of it consumed by youngsters.

Drissa is a child but does not care for chocolate so much. He still carries the marks of his time working on a cocoa plantation in the Ivory Coast. Numerous wounds from beatings adorn his back. Some are down to the bone.

Drissa was a 'chocolate slave', one of an unknown number of children from West Africa sold by their families into bondage in the Ivory Coast, the world's largest producer of cocoa. They are paid nothing, beaten into submission and abandoned when illness makes them useless.

Drissa worked 18 hours a day on little food and was locked in a small room at night. The beatings, rather than wages, provided his incentive. The 'chocolate slaves' used in the Ivory Coast are said to come mainly from Mali, Benin, Togo and the Central African Republic but information is scant.

Unicef believes between 10,000 and 15,000 children are working on the plantations on the Ivory Coast although it is not known how many are there illegally. Cocoa prices dropped to a 30-year low last year and unpaid labour is tempting in an industry where prices are barely matching the production costs.

Mali and the Ivory Coast at least paid lip service to the slave trade when they signed an agreement in September banning the trafficking in children. Britain's chocolate industry, however, denies that the child slave problem exists at all.

Following a television documentary last year exposing the plight of Drissa and the chocolate slaves, the industry body, the Biscuit, Cake, Chocolate and Confectionery

Alliance, commissioned an inquiry. The research body it chose discovered no direct evidence of slave use in the chocolate industry although its report admitted that conditions existed to allow it.

The alliance said: 'It is quite wrong to imply that slavery is either widespread or representative of conditions generally on cocoa farms. Members of our industry and the cocoa processors have been visiting the Ivory Coast for decades and working closely with many cocoa farmers. In all that time, we simply have not come across such practices. That is why we are confident that, while illegal practices may exist, this is on a very limited scale indeed and confined to certain areas.'

They are paid nothing, beaten into submission and abandoned when illness makes them useless

---

But as the alliance admits, there are more than one million cocoa farms in the Ivory Coast. A spokesman for Cadbury's said that very little of the chocolate in British confectionery used cocoa from the Ivory Coast. Ninety per cent came from Ghana. However, with the Ivory Coast dominating the market, a large proportion of chocolate imported into Britain must come from there.

Industry denials did not convince Brian Wilson, Foreign Office minister, who urged manufacturers to ensure their products were free from ingredients connected to child slavery. 'It does seem that the use of slave child labour in cocoa plantations in some countries is common,' he told Radio 4's *Today* programme.

He added: 'In West Africa, the only countries which have signed the International Labour Organisation convention on the elimination of the worst forms of child labour are Togo, Ghana and Senegal. I believe that certainly large, reputable British manufacturers would use cocoa which comes from countries with plantations where there are relatively good conditions.

'But I would ask everybody involved in the trade in Britain to be absolutely sure that they are not using raw materials produced in areas where there is child labour. We are all entitled to ask every confectioner and cocoa manufacturer that the source of their product is ethically produced.'

• By Neil Tweedie

Warning over child slave trade

Thousands of west African children are being traded in Britain as domestic slaves by people who use them to claim benefits, social workers have warned.

They said the slave trade was coordinated by criminal gangs who often took children from their parents in lieu of debts incurred from being smuggled into the UK.

The situation has come to light in the wake of the inquiry into the death of child abuse victim Victoria Climbié, who was murdered after being sent from the Ivory Coast to live with her great-aunt. The eight-year-old died at her north Tottenham home in February 2000 after suffering 128 separate injuries.

A BBC investigation identified a network of 13 adults who ran a child-trading network in London.

One woman in north-west London had acquired 12 children, for each of which she was able to claim £40 a week in benefits.

It emerged that three of these had since been taken into care, care orders were out on three more, two had been passed on to a south London woman and two were missing.

'Children are being trafficked and held hostage in lieu of debt repayments and in doing so are being abused, being used as houseboys or servants and younger children are being neglected,' said an unnamed social worker.

'In my 15-year career in social work, inside and outside London, I have come across it in every place I have worked,' he said.

The social worker added that social service departments lacked the legal powers to investigate cases while the police did not have sufficient resources.

Trafficked children could be located through the benefit system, but inspectors were interested only in checking that multiple claims were not being made for the same child and not in whether the child was with its legitimate carer, he claimed.

The trafficking network extends to Ireland, making it even more difficult for the authorities to track down the child slaves.

'From a point of view of trying to identify whether these children are being used, it is virtually impossible,' said an Irish health-worker, who also wished to remain anonymous.

'They disappear and go back to the UK. There is a network between the UK and Ireland.'

Esther Rantzen, founder and chairwoman of ChildLine, said social services should investigate child-trafficking 'as a matter of urgency'.

'It is quite clear that social workers do have evidence of what is going on and have taken children into care,' she said.

However, Ms Rantzen expressed concern that some social workers were reluctant to pursue possible cases because of 'politically correct' beliefs that passing children around extended families was simply part of west African culture.

Mike Caye, communications director of charity Anti-Slavery International, said legislation was needed to deal with human trafficking for both sexual and labour exploitation.

'Until you get the legislation in place, you can't make it a priority for the police,' he warned. In a statement, the Home Office said: 'Trafficking of human beings, and particularly children, is an abhorrent practice.

'The UK signed the trafficking protocol of the UN convention on transnational organised crime and there is at European level a draft framework for the definition of trafficking in human beings.'

© Guardian Newspapers Limited 2001

Child labour in the shadow of the World Cup

With only 5 months left until the 2002 FIFA World Cup kicks off in Japan and Korea, activists from around the world are putting increasing pressure on FIFA and national football teams to make this championship the first international sporting event free of child labour and in compliance with fair labour standards. This international campaign has been initiated by the Global March Against Child Labour.

India and Pakistan are the largest football producers for the world football championship. According to a recent report by the India Committee of the Netherlands and the All Pakistan Federation of Labour (APFL), thousands of children in Pakistan and India are involved in the production of footballs. Moreover, workers in both countries are earning wages much lower than the legal minimum wage and many basic labour rights are routinely neglected. Their life of exploitation is shared by another 250 million working children around the world and many of their families.

Recently, a team from the Global March left for Jalandhar, in the Indian State of Punjab, and captured pictures of children as young as 10 years old stitching footballs.

'I have been stitching footballs for as long as I can remember,' confided Geeta, a young girl from Jalandhar who estimated her age to be between 10 and 12 years old. 'My hands are constantly in pain. It feels like they are burning. There is nothing I can do—I have to help my older sister complete the order.'

Most children are forced into labour to help their families earn enough money to survive. Hence, football stitching becomes home-based family work where a middleman, who acts on behalf of a sporting goods manufacturer, provides the football pieces for in-home production. A normal working day does not often provide the workers with even

January 2002, New Delhi

the legal minimum wage. While helping their families, many of the children miss out on their education, creating a vicious circle of poverty and uneducated labour.

Mohan Lal, a local stitcher, said that his own children and neighbours' children were involved in stitching footballs for the 2002 World Cup. He maintained, however, that children were not involved in the production of sporting gloves.

In 1998 FIFA established a Code of Conduct to prohibit the use of child labour and to require decent working conditions and wages for adult workers in all FIFA-licensed products. However, available evidence points to routine violations of the Code by the manufacturers.

In response to Global March's enquiries last May, Michel Zen-Ruffinen, General Secretary of FIFA, in an official letter dated 7 December 2001, declared that 'it is not correct to say that there are no monitoring systems in place, although we have been in talks with our partners in the last two weeks to improve this aspect of the project'. He also affirmed that all football and referee equipment is produced in full conformity with the current labour standards.

The Global March acknowledges the efforts by sporting goods producers and ILO-IPEC in Sialkot, Pakistan, which establishes a monitoring system for football production and provides education

opportunities for children. 'In India, an industry-led monitoring system exists, however it lacks transparency as there is no public information about its functioning or results,' says Gerard Oonk, author of *The Dark Side of Football* report on labour conditions in the football industry in Punjab, India published in 2001. Oonk also says that in other countries where footballs and sporting goods are manufactured, such as China, there is no credible monitoring system in place. None of the current monitoring systems enforces key labour rights for adult workers, most notably wages.

'A game that is supposed to inspire youth and entertain the world must not be played with footballs sewn with the sweat of children. Children must be given pens to study and toys to play,' said Kailash Satyarthi, Chairperson of the Global March.

To celebrate the Global March Anniversary, as part of the World Cup Campaign 2002, football stars will be participating in a friendly game with child labourers in South Africa and Japan will be hosting a public discussion on the appeals made to the Planning Committee of the World Cup to take child labour out of the game. Internationally, an online petition campaign calling on FIFA to fully implement their Code of Conduct will be launched at www.globalmarch.org, reaching out to thousands of youth and football fans to voice their opinions for fair play.

The World Cup Campaign is one of the main campaigns led by the Global March in the year 2002. The movement was born out of a foot-march that commenced four years ago today, when thousands of people took a journey over 80,000 kilometres, in four continents to mobilise worldwide action against the worst forms of child labour. Some 2,000 partners in over 140 countries have joined the movement.

© Global March Against Child Labour

Solutions to child labour

Information from World Vision

Introduction

Whilst child labourers are in many ways victims of the development process they are also active participants within it. Reflecting this, the world's working children are increasingly demanding that others listen to their rights as workers and children. In many poor countries there are moves to fight for the right of children to work under decent conditions.

As a development agency concerned with ensuring that the best interests of the child (as outlined in the United Nations Convention on the Rights of the Child) are met, this is a challenging and at times seemingly contradictory process. For World Vision, the answer lies in finding the balance between the protection of children and the participation of children in change.

Fatal cures: the problem of punitive solutions

World Vision has seen first hand the devastating results which can occur when attempts are made to eradicate all child work immediately. In recognising the evident problem of exploitative child labour, non-government organisations, governments and commercial organisations must avoid the automatic but understandable temptation to require the instant prohibition of all child labour.

Well-meaning measures can often have disastrous consequences, an example has been provided by experience following an Act introduced into Congress in America. The Act was designed to penalise industries found to be using child labour through sanctions, an approach favoured by protectionist labour unions and advocated by President Clinton at the Seattle WTO meeting. The originator of the Bill, Senator Tom Harkin, said, 'As importers and consumers of products made by exploitative forms of child labour, we must not co-

operate in perpetuating abroad a practice we abhor in our own land.' When the Child Labour Deterrence Act was first introduced into Congress it led to preventative action by factory owners who faced being penalised, particularly in Bangladesh, one of the largest garment suppliers to the US. Those factories which feared the loss of US contracts, dismissed an estimated 70,000 child workers.[1]

A follow-up study by Oxfam found that an estimated 30,000 children who formerly worked in the garment industry in Bangladesh have now moved into the more hazardous welding and sex industries. Now that the Child Labour Deterrence Act has been passed, many more child factory workers may be forced out of their jobs into more hazardous industries, or they may be forced into underground factories where there are no means of monitoring working conditions.[2]

Belatedly the ILO was able to bring together factory owners, workers' groups and NGOs to implement education projects and income assistance initiatives for the

families involved. The lesson of the Harkin Bill, however, was that while families continue to live in poverty with an over-riding need for income, their children are open to exploitation. If children are not sent into export industry factories to work, they may well be sent to work in other less monitorable industries. Indeed, most child labourers are found on farms, in households, on the streets and in informal workshops where they are normally beyond the reach of protective labour legislation.

As a result of Harkin and other instances of punitive action World Vision does not favour consumer boycotts or sanctions. Instead World Vision has consistently advocated a multi-pronged approach as highlighted through a series of World Vision and World Vision funded publications, including: *Offering Hope not Despair*, *Helping Business to Help Stop Child Labour* and *The Commercial Sexual Exploitation of Street Children*. This approach can be summarised as:

- Ending the worst forms of child labour quickly
- Persuading formal sector employers to improve conditions and shorten hours
- Creating income alternatives for families

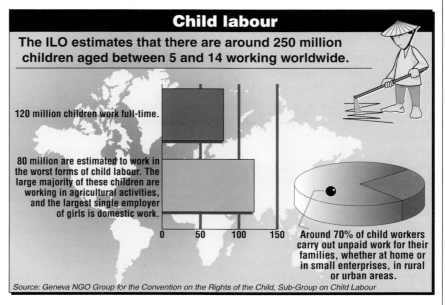

Child labour

The ILO estimates that there are around 250 million children aged between 5 and 14 working worldwide.

120 million children work full-time.

80 million are estimated to work in the worst forms of child labour. The large majority of these children are working in agricultural activities, and the largest single employer of girls is domestic work.

0   50   100   150

Around 70% of child workers carry out unpaid work for their families, whether at home or in small enterprises, in rural or urban areas.

Source: Geneva NGO Group for the Convention on the Rights of the Child, Sub-Group on Child Labour

- Improving access to good quality and appropriate education
- Tackling the structural impediments which create and compound poverty

These changes are only possible if long-term, structural changes are pursued.

The long-term issues

The underlying causes of child labour are basically structural – widespread poverty, gross inequality, income distribution, poor or inadequate education, malnutrition, unjust land distribution, the status of women, structures of countries' economies, consumer patterns, as well as macro-economic policy frameworks. In addition, the implementation of some Structural Adjustment Pro-grammes, imposed by the International Monetary Fund onto developing states, has diverted funds from areas such as health and education. The provision of basic education and primary health are fundamental to tackling poverty. This reality exists alongside falling aid levels from major donors and is not conducive to the fight against exploitative child labour.

The elimination of all child labour will require that these issues are addressed. Development projects which aim to tackle the inequities of child labour must also address national and international, political, social and economic inequalities. This is not to say that poverty automatically leads to poor children entering the workforce, but it does create the conditions which make it likely. Indeed the reasons children are preferred to adult workers can be of a non-economic nature. Children are less aware of their rights, they accept repetitive and dangerous work more readily and are more obedient. Children are easier to exploit. Nevertheless the dramatic rise in the numbers of working children in Indonesia following the economic crisis were indicative of the income-labour dynamic.

Where children do work, and structural conditions exist which perpetuate child labour then the interests of the children involved may be best served by encouraging employers to end exploitative practices without automatically discarding child workers.

This type of transitional approach moves children out of exploitative labour and into non-exploitative labour. Such a strategy entails the implementation of adequate health and safety conditions within work environments, as well as appropriate hours, nutrition and the provision of some form of education and skills training. The transitional approach may be particularly relevant for older children (13 years) who have never attended school and who may be better served learning new skills, coupled with a vocational education rather than being sent to a classroom.

But even this strategy must only form a small part of a much more comprehensive approach to child labour. Prevention, removal and rehabilitation should be the three pillars of any strategy to eliminate child labour. Of these, prevention can be the most difficult, often focusing on long-term, international, national, community and family based solutions. These are, however, imperative for any successful programme to eliminate child labour.

It is possible to eradicate child labour. In the short term we should aim at eradicating the most extreme forms of exploitative labour

---

In Latin America, local non-government organisations estimate that up to a third of all family income is generated from child labour. More broadly, some evidence suggests that children in poor families can sometimes contribute up to a quarter of a household's income. Instantly removing children from work without providing sustainable alternatives for both them and their families may well drive many further into poverty.

Education the answer?

One of the keys to both the prevention and cure of exploitative child labour is education. Education alone is not enough to end the abuse of children, but as part of a broader programme aimed at reducing poverty and the other pressures that drive children into work, it is imperative.

Education, to be effective in combating child labour, must be compulsory, allow equal access for boys and girls, be of high quality, be relevant, be free, and it should be realistically flexible to allow for farming seasons and its associated demands. It must also have minimal out-of-pocket costs. For example IPEC has estimated that globally out-of-pocket costs for a primary school education can represent up to a third of cash income for a typical poor family.

In addition to being affordable for even the poorest families, education must be of good quality. It must be meaningful and equip children with skills for future employment. In areas with high child labour and high school drop-out rates it is often found that the education is of a poor standard. Inappropriate education can inadvertently prompt children to go to work, where they may learn skills and earn an income.

It is possible to eradicate child labour. In the short term we should aim at eradicating the most extreme forms of exploitative labour. Over the longer term, governments, consumers, child rights groups and child labourers, should work together to ensure that all children have the opportunity to have their full development potential realised and their fundamental human rights met.

References
1 World Vision staff, 'Eradicating Child Labour Without Putting Children on the Streets', *Together – A Journal of the World Vision Partnership*, No. 58, April-June, pp.9-10.
2 Ibid.

• The above information is an extract from World Vision's web site: www.worldvision.org.uk

Commercial sexual exploitation

Facts and figures

Because the commercial sexual exploitation of children is largely hidden, accurate data on its occurrence are difficult to collect. When surveys do exist, definitions of child prostitution and sexual exploitation vary. Some estimates include street children who may sell sex if someone makes an offer; others include children working only in brothels or massage parlours, where many are kept in a state indistinguishable from slavery. Even though incomplete, the data show a serious problem.

- In Lithuania, 20 to 50 per cent of prostitutes are believed to be minors. Children as young as age 11 are known to work as brothel prostitutes, and children from children's homes, some 10 to 12 years old, have been used to make pornographic movies.
- In Cambodia, in a Human Rights Vigilance survey of 6,110 sex workers in the city of Phnom Penh and in 11 provinces, 31 per cent of those interviewed were children aged 12 to 17.
- Debt bondage is often the way girls enter prostitution in many Asian countries, including India, Myanmar, Nepal, Pakistan and Thailand. The girl must work off the money given to parents or a guardian and cannot leave prostitution until the debt is fully paid. Girls make little money, and expenses such as rent, transportation and food are added to the debt, making it extremely difficult to pay off.
- A study conducted in the United States revealed that one in five children who go online regularly are approached by strangers for sex. A separate study revealed

United Nations Children's Fund

that an estimated 104,000 children become victims of sexual abuse each year.
- In Thailand, close to $300 million is estimated to be transferred annually from urban to rural areas by women working in the sex trade in urban areas.
- A Pakistani study found that, based only on reported cases, at least one rape incident involving a woman or child occurs on

average every three hours in Pakistan.
- Research involving advanced secondary and university students in Sri Lanka revealed that 12 per cent of girls said they had experienced sexual abuse as children, and that even more boys – 20 per cent – said they had. Girls avoided divulging to the researchers their relationship to the perpetrators. Boys most often said it was a family member.
- In south-eastern Europe, women and children are often trafficked through the same routes used to smuggle drugs and arms.
- According to a survey by *India Today* magazine, there are between 400,000 and 500,000 child prostitutes in India.
- In Mexico, a study of six cities (Acapulco, Cancún, Ciudad Juarez, Guadalajara, Tapachula and Tijuana) estimated that a total of 4,600 children are sexually exploited in these cities. At the national level, some 16,000 children are believed to be exploited.
- From 1996 to 1998, girls aged 17 and under constituted approximately 40 per cent of reported rape and attempted rape victims in South Africa. Twenty per cent of young women surveyed in Johannesburg reported a history of sexual abuse by the age of 18.

• The above information is an extract from *Profiting from Abuse – An investigation into the sexual exploitation of our children*, produced by UNICEF. Alternatively, see page 41 for their address details,

Sexual exploitation

Protection of children from sexual exploitation

Laws are being made world-wide to prevent and punish sexual offenders who commit these crimes outside their own countries (sexual tourism). Foreigners and citizens alike should not be exempt from following the United Nations Convention on the Rights of the Child's laws concerning the safety and well-being of children.

- The commercial sexual exploitation of children is estimated to be a multi-billion dollar industry, drawing in over 1 million children each year worldwide.
- The 'sex tourism' industry, involving men travelling to other countries to engage in sex with children, has been documented in the Philippines, Cambodia, Thailand, and countries in North America and Eastern Europe. Most of the children exploited in the sex trade are between the ages of 13 and 18, although there is evidence of children younger than 5 being sexually exploited as well.
- Asia is the worst affected area for child prostitution, in which one million children are sexually exploited. There are an estimated 30,000 children in India in the sex trade, and between 80,000 and 800,000 children in Thailand.
- Approximately 30% of the 185,000 prostitutes in Vietnam are thought to be under the age of 16.
- In Latin America, approximately 25,400 children are engaged in prostitution in the Dominican Republic, and 3,000 children were sexually exploited in Colombia's capital, Bogota, alone.

> *The commercial sexual exploitation of children is estimated to be a multi-billion dollar industry, drawing in over 1 million children each year worldwide*

- A recent survey indicated an estimated 5,000 children are involved in prostitution, pornography, and sex tourism in Mexico, most of whom are street children.
- In Africa, sexual exploitation of children is on the rise in the whole continent. In South Africa, of the country's 40 million people, 70,000 women and girls are believed to be working in the sex trade.
- In Africa, young boys are often recruited into the armed forces not only to fight, but also to sexually service the soldiers.
- A large portion of child prostitutes catch sexually transmitted diseases (including HIV/AIDS), are forced to have abortions, and suffer serious psychological problems.
- One study found that 60 to 70% of child prostitutes in Thailand are HIV infected.
- Many circumstances such as poverty, lack of education, and parental pressure force children into the sex industry. Many families, however, mistakenly send their children into what they believe to be domestic servitude, where the children are then kidnapped, trafficked across borders, and forced to work as sex slaves.

© Source Unattributable

Sexual abuse and exploitation

Information from Human Rights Watch

'When they brought me here, it was in a taxi. I kept looking around, wondering what kind of work was going on in this area of this big city. Everywhere I looked, I saw curtained doorways and rooms. Men would go and come through these curtained entrances. People on the street would be calling out, "Two rupees, two rupees." I asked the other Nepali women if these were offices; it seemed the logical explanation. In two days I knew everything. I cried.'

Tara N., a Nepali woman who was trafficked into India at sixteen.

Children around the world are sexually abused and exploited in ways that can cause permanent physical and psychological harm. In some cases, police demand sexual services from street children, threatening them with arrest if they do not comply. In detention and correctional facilities children may be sexually abused by staff or are not protected from sexual abuse by other inmates. In refugee camps many children are exploited by adults or sometimes forced to sell their bodies for food. Children in orphanages may be abused by staff members or other children. In conflict areas children are kidnapped to serve as child soldiers and also as sexual servants for adult soldiers. Children working as domestics may be assaulted or raped by employers.

This grim picture is compounded by the use of children as prostitutes in countries throughout the world. An unknown but very large number of children are used for commercial sexual purposes every year, often ending up with their health destroyed, victims of HIV/AIDS and other sexually transmitted diseases. Younger and younger children are sought with the expectation that clients will not be exposed to HIV. Prostituted children can be raped, beaten, sodomised, emotionally abused, tortured, and even killed by pimps, brothel owners, and

customers. Some have been trafficked from one country to another; both boys and girls are trafficked. Moreover, child prostitutes are frequently treated as criminals by law enforcement and judicial authorities, rather than as children who are victims of sexual exploitation.

Articles 34 and 35 of the Convention on the Rights of the Child forbid sexual exploitation or trafficking of children, and the Committee on the Rights of the Child has devoted time and efforts to the issue, urging governments to crack down on the practice. Other international instruments in human rights, humanitarian law, refugee law, and labour standards protect children against sexual exploitation. In addition, a UN special rapporteur on the sale of children, child prostitution and child pornography investigates these issues.

> **In conflict areas children are kidnapped to serve as child soldiers and also as sexual servants for adult soldiers. Children working as domestics may be assaulted or raped by employers**

A good deal of international attention has been focused on sexual exploitation and trafficking, particularly on the practice of sex tourism, which is a relatively small part of the problem. A World Congress against Commercial Sexual Exploitation of Children was held in Stockholm in 1996, attended by representatives of governments, UN bodies, and non-governmental organisations, from 125 countries. The congress issued a strong declaration against commercial sexual exploitation of children and an agenda for action; an international focal point on sexual exploitation of children was established in Geneva to coordinate reform efforts. A number of governments and NGOs are continuing their efforts to attack the problem. But vast numbers of children are still trapped in this life-threatening sex trade.

Human Rights Watch has investigated the trafficking of women and girls from Burma to Thailand and from Nepal to India. In 1993 we found that many girls were among the thousands of Burmese trafficked into Thai brothels every year. They worked in conditions tantamount to slavery. Subject to debt bondage, illegal confinement, various forms of sexual and physical abuse, and exposure to HIV in brothels, they then faced arrest as illegal immigrants if they tried to escape or if the brothels were raided by Thai police. Once arrested, the girls were sometimes subjected to further sexual abuse in Thai detention centres. They were then taken to the Thai-Burmese border where they were often lured back into prostitution by brothel agents who played on their fear of arrest on return to Burma. Thai police and border patrol officials were involved in both the trafficking and the brothel operations, but they routinely escaped punishment as do, for the most part, brothel agents, pimps and clients.

In 1995 we looked into the trafficking of Nepali women and girls to brothels in India. The victims of this international trafficking network routinely suffered serious physical abuse, including rape, beatings, arbitrary imprisonment and exposure to HIV/AIDS. Held in debt bondage for years at a time, girls worked under constant surveillance. Escape was virtually impossible. Both the Indian and Nepali governments were complicit in the abuses. Police and officials in India protected brothel owners and traffickers in return for bribes; Nepali border police accepted bribes to allow trafficking. Even when traffickers were identified, few arrests and even fewer prosecutions resulted.

The international community, both governments and non-governmental groups, must make every effort to end these abuses. In some cases new laws are required; in others the political will must be mobilized to implement existing legislation and prosecute those involved in sexually abusing and exploiting these vulnerable children.

Recommendations

1 Governments must implement the Stockholm Agenda for Action to which they agreed during the World Congress against Commercial Sexual Exploitation, and prosecute those who abuse and sexually exploit children, or profit from the practice.

2 Children engaged in prostitution must be treated as victims of sexual exploitation, violence, and forced labour, and not as criminals. Governments and aid groups should support quality rehabilitation and recovery programmes for children who leave the sex trade, which include psychological counselling, health care, education and vocational training, and shelter, as appropriate.

3 Governments must develop prevention programmes that will raise public awareness and encourage actions that protect children.

• The above information is an extract from *Promises Broken – An Assessment of Children's Rights on the 10th Anniversary of the Convention on the Rights of the Child*, produced by Human Rights Watch. Visit their web site at www.hrw.org or see page 41 for their postal address details.
© 2001, Human Rights Watch

Sexual exploitation of children

Information from ECPAT UK (End Child Prostitution, Child Pornography And the Trafficking of children for sexual purposes)

What is the commercial sexual exploitation of children?
It happens to children world-wide. It is the sexual abuse of a child by an adult paid for either by cash or in kind (through meals, clothes, payment of rent etc.). The three main elements are:
- child prostitution
- child pornography
- the trafficking and sale of children for sexual purposes

Why should we take action?
- Because Britons are amongst those who sexually exploit children overseas
- Prostitution is a death sentence for many children. STDs (sexually transmitted diseases) and AIDS/HIV, to which children are more susceptible, are rampant in the sex industries
- Children suffer tremendous physical and emotional pain as a result of prostitution
- Prostituted children are victims not criminals
- Every child, however poor, has the right not to be treated as a sexual commodity

'Children and young people are not commodities. They are not merely statistics or even cases. They are the link between us and the future. They are that future. We cannot fail them.'
Jo de Linde, Chair of ECPAT International

Who are the children?
They are both boys and girls aged up to 18 years, though the majority are girls. They generally come from poor, rural families or are homeless children living on the streets. Many are sold by family or friends, tricked or abducted into prostitution. Some children may simply have no other option but to prostitute themselves in order to survive.

Why are children sexually exploited?
The root causes are complex. Poverty, lack of opportunities for education or employment, homelessness, criminal networks and family breakdown are all important factors. Children from minority ethnic groups are particularly vulnerable, as are girls who are often seen as less 'important' than boys. Children are also increasingly seen as commodities in a global market who can be bought or sold.

• The above is an extract from ECPAT UK's web site which can be found at www.ecpat.org.uk Alternatively, see page 41 for their address details.
© *ECPAT UK (End Child Prostitution, Child Pornography And the Trafficking of children for sexual purposes)*

Sex trafficking of children still not a crime

Nearly 200 years after the abolition of slavery in the UK, people trafficking, including the sale of children for sexual exploitation, still exists. Christian Aid-funded Ecpat UK – End Child Prostitution, Pornography and Trafficking – is calling for new legislation, and better support for the victims of this 21st-century slave trade.

Jane was just 15 when, under the threat of death from a voodoo curse, she was trafficked from her native Nigeria to the UK, with the intention of selling her into sexual slavery in Europe. Fortunately, as she was being taken from Britain to Germany by another member of the trafficking ring, she was picked up by the police, who did not believe the story she had been forced to tell: that she was 28. Unfortunately they let the trafficker go, while Jane spent five months in a detention centre.

Jane's story is not unusual in the murky world of trafficking, a form of modern-day slavery. Although the police have good intentions when trying to deal with the problem of children being brought into this country for illegal purposes, child trafficking is still not recognised as a criminal offence. The only tool available to prosecutors is the 44-year-old Sexual Offences Act. In practice if not in theory, the maximum sentence under this act is one and a half to two years in jail. This is a poor deterrent for a business which can net hundreds of thousands of pounds each year for the people behind it.

Now Ecpat UK (End Child Prostitution, Pornography and Trafficking), funded by Christian Aid, has just carried out the first ever research into the sexual trafficking of children into the UK, and is calling for new legislation to be brought in as a matter of priority.

'What we want is the introduction of adequate legislation relating to trafficking and the seriousness of the crime. But what is also needed is adequate protection and support of trafficked children,' says Carron Somerset, the report's author.

The children, mostly from west Africa, and predominantly Nigeria, often arrive accompanied by an adult posing as a relative. They declare themselves asylum seekers, but are quickly identified as being under age, and taken into care. It is from the care home that they escape, into the arms of the trafficker.

There are, however, many other routes for the trafficking. Although Ecpat UK found no empirical proof that children are being brought in from eastern Europe there is strong anecdotal evidence which points to this as another serious problem.

Although the police have good intentions when trying to deal with the problem of children being brought into this country for illegal purposes, child trafficking is still not recognised as a criminal offence

---

Although it is difficult to gauge the precise scale of the problem, figures from West Sussex Social Services (which picks up many of the children who fly into Gatwick) provide a good indicator: 66 young people have gone missing from its care since 1995, the majority of whom, it may be assumed, have gone to their trafficker to be pimped out.

'There are many reasons why children are trafficked. They include poverty, lack of employment opportunities, discrimination within the culture and instability within sending countries due to conflict. But in many cases trafficking victims do go willingly with the trafficker, either because their parents have told them they must, or because they think they will end up with a better life,' says Ms Somerset.

They are also persuaded to co-operate with their captors because of voodoo. Like Jane, many west African children are put under a curse in their home country. Ceremonies, during which locks of the child's hair are taken, or a live chicken is cut, trap the juvenile into the trafficking deal. They are told that if they escape, their bodies will swell up and they will die.

Ms Somerset emphasises that this report is just the beginning of the research which must be commissioned if trafficking patterns are to be understood and intercepted:

'Throughout the research it became apparent that children can be trafficked into the UK, with little chance of being detected by the authorities. What about children being brought in by a "relative" who states they are bringing the child in for educational reasons? . . . No one knows how many children are in the UK and could be at risk of sexual exploitation,' she says.

Aside from sexual exploitation, it is believed that young people are also brought in to act as drug smugglers, perpetrate credit card fraud and to be forced into marriage.

Ecpat is also calling for safe houses for children once they have been identified by the police or social services and for counselling for the young victims. Mike Kaye of campaign group Anti-Slavery International endorses this: 'This should not be seen as a wish list, but be seen as essential to combating the trafficking of children.'

• The above information is from Christian Aid's web site which can be found at www.christian-aid.org.uk Alternatively see page 41 for their address details.

© Christian Aid

British sex tourists

British tourists in the top five most likely to buy sex from children in Cambodia

Holidaying Britons are amongst the main culprits for buying sex from children in Cambodia according to a report launched today by World Vision, an international aid and development agency.

The report says that British men rank fifth in a list of nationalities most involved with child sex tourism, along with Chinese men, Frenchmen, Americans and Germans.

World Vision's report, *Child's Work, Adults' Play: Child Sex Tourism, a Problem in Cambodia*, is being launched to coincide with the Second World Congress Against Commercial Sexual Exploitation of Children held in Yokohama, Japan between 17 -20 December 2001.

The report carried out in conjunction with the Cambodian Ministry of Tourism and the Cambodia National Council of Children shows a devastating picture of official complicity, active promotion of the problem by the industry, and systematic and accepted sexual violence against boys and girls.

Laurence Gray, World Vision's manager for Children in Especially Difficult Circumstances in Cambodia, and author of the report, said,

World Vision

'Sex tourists are attracted to economically poor countries by factors that include low-cost prostitution, wide availability and perceived immunity from prosecution. With 65 per cent of tourists visiting Cambodia in 2000 being men, the country has been increasingly linked to child prostitution.'

> *British men rank fifth in a list of nationalities most involved with child sex tourism, along with Chinese men, Frenchmen, Americans and Germans*

The report lends weight to World Vision's call on the UK government to change legislation to force sex offenders convicted overseas to register when they return to the UK.

The aid and development agency, a member of ECPAT (End Child Prostitution, Pornography and Trafficking) commends the government for its action following the first world congress on Commercial Sexual Exploitation of Children five years ago in Stockholm. Here 124 countries signed up to develop national action plans to tackle the issue in 1996 but only 34 countries have carried this out, to their credit, the UK and Cambodia are two of these.

In 2000 the UK published the amendments to the Sex Offenders Act 1997 requiring that sex offenders give notice to the police at least 24 hours before they leave the UK. Currently British nationals convicted overseas for sex offences do have to register when they return to the UK but the implementation of this may prove problematic if information is not forthcoming.

• The above information is an extract from World Vision's web site: www.worldvision.org.uk Alternatively, see page 41 for their address details.

© *World Vision*

Debunking the myths

Information from UNICEF

Sexual abuse of children occurs when a child is used as an object of sexual gratification for an older or more knowledgeable child or adult (a stranger, sibling or person in a position of authority, such as a parent or caregiver). These contacts or interactions are often carried out against the child using force, trickery, bribes, threats or pressure. Sexual abuse can be physical, verbal or emotional.

Commercial sexual exploitation is the use of a child for sexual purposes in exchange for cash or favours between the customer, intermediary or agent and other who profit from the trade in children for these purposes (parent, family member, procurer, teacher). The United Nations refers to three forms of commercial sexual exploitation of children; child prostitution; trafficking and sale of children across borders and within countries for sexual purposes; and child pornography.

Perpetrators benefits from the myths surrounding sexual abuse and commercial sexual exploitation to lure and recruit children.

Myth: Child sexual abuse and commercial sexual exploitation are not a widespread problem.

Fact: Most sexual abuse of children never comes to the attention of government authorities. Secrecy and intense feelings of shame may prevent children – and adults aware of the abuse – from seeking help. Existing studies present a disturbing picture:

- Research with advanced secondary and university students in Sri Lanka revealed that 12 per cent of girls and 20 per cent of boys said they had experienced sexual abuse as children.
- In a research study carried out in Kingston (Jamaica), it was reported that among 450 schoolchildren between the ages of 13 and 14, 13 per cent had experienced attempted rape.

unicef
United Nations Children's Fund

- In a national study of runaway and homeless youth in the United States, 17 per cent of homeless youth surveyed had been forced into unwanted sexual activity by a family or household member.

There are no adequately documented figures on the number of children who are sexually exploited for commercial purposes.

> *Commercial sexual exploitation is the use of a child for sexual purposes in exchange for cash or favours between the customer, intermediary or agent and other who profit from the trade in children for these purposes*

The clandestine nature of the international sex industry has made it impossible to move beyond broad estimates.

- Approximately 1 million children enter the sex trade every year.
- Asia Watch, a non-governmental organisation (NGO), has reported that as many as 50,000 Nepalese girls have been sold and trafficked to India as bonded labour in Bombay brothels.
- There are an estimated 25,000 child sex workers in the Dominican Republic.
- In West Africa, an estimated 35,000 children are sex workers.

Myth: Only girls are exposed to sexual exploitation.

Fact: Although the majority of sexually abused and exploited children are girls, boys are also victims. The sexual abuse of boys is less frequently reported than the abuse of girls and has received less recognition. Because many societies expect boys and men to be in control of their emotions, other people and their environment, it is particularly difficult for boys to disclose that they have been sexually assaulted. Adolescent boys who are targeted by other men may feel that their

manhood and sexual orientation will be called into question if they reveal the abuse. Adolescent boys who are targeted by older females may not view the sexual contact as abusive.

Myth: Child sexual exploitation is a recent phenomenon largely initiated by sex tourists.
Fact: The international media has brought a great of attention to sex tourism, but child sexual exploitation has a long history, with most abuse perpetrated by members of the local community.

Myth: Sex exploiters are all paedophiles and strangers.
Fact: Male paedophiles are among the abusers, but most abusers are 'situational' offenders, who, at times of stress, or out of convenience or curiosity, engage in sexual activity with children. A majority of sexually abused who are not involved in commercial sexual activity are abused by someone they know: parents, step-parents, teachers, doctors, relatives, clergy and neighbours.

Myth: Sex with a virgin or a young child may prevent or cure HIV/ AIDS.
Fact: Children trapped in prostitution are actually at a greater risk of contracting sexually transmitted infections (STIs), including HIV/ AIDS, than adults are. Their developing bodies make them less able to resist dominance and more vulnerable to the injuries of aggression.

Myth: Children in prostitution choose this profession.
Fact: Children cannot choose to be involved in prostitution. They are forced into it by circumstances, are coerced, tricked or abducted, or have fled from situations of abuse and neglect. Many have a history of sexual abuse that has left them with feelings of helplessness, low self-esteem and an unhealthy perspective about sexuality.

Myth: Sexual exploitation of children is caused by poverty.
Fact: Poverty creates conditions that can contribute to sexual exploitation, but poverty alone is not a reason why children are sold into commercial

sex. In poor communities, there is generally a high rate of illiteracy and a lack of marketable skills. These conditions make it easier for procurement agents to obtain children for the sex trade from urban slums and poor rural villages. Family breakdown, globalisation, local culture, the low status of women and weak law enforcement all contribute to the exploitation of children. Some families hand over their children to agents or middlemen with full knowledge of what will happen. At times, this is to relieve poverty; at other times, the family is seeking additional material gain.

Myth: Sexual abuse of children is not always damaging.
Fact: Sexual abuse of children is an act of violence. Even if there are no physical injuries, there is always psychological damage. Children who are sexually abused are denied a childhood and betrayed by a person who is in a position of authority and trust.

Sexual abuse and exploitation can take place anywhere. The offenders come from all social groups and races, and education and income levels

---

Myth: The effects of sexual abuse are clear and evident.
Fact: Physical evidence of sexual abuse is rare. Because most children cannot or do not tell about being sexually abused, it is up to concerned adults to recognise signs of abuse. Unfortunately, there is no single behaviour that proves that a child has been sexually abused. Such children may exhibit a wide range of behaviours, including: difficulty concentrating in school; withdrawal from family and friends; sleep disturbances; depression; irritability; a sudden loss of or increase in appetite; aggressiveness; inappropriate sexual play with peers, toys or themselves; signs of regression like thumb-sucking, bed-wetting or acting like an infant; and alcohol and drug use.

Myth: Child victims come from poor families.
Fact: Sexual abuse and exploitation can take place anywhere. The offenders come from all social groups and races, and education and income levels. Middle and upper-class families, however, are more capable of hiding the abuse and its consequences.

• The above information is an extract from *Profiting from Abuse – An investigation into the sexual exploitation of our children*, produced by UNICEF. See page 41 for their address details,

Child trafficking for purposes of prostitution

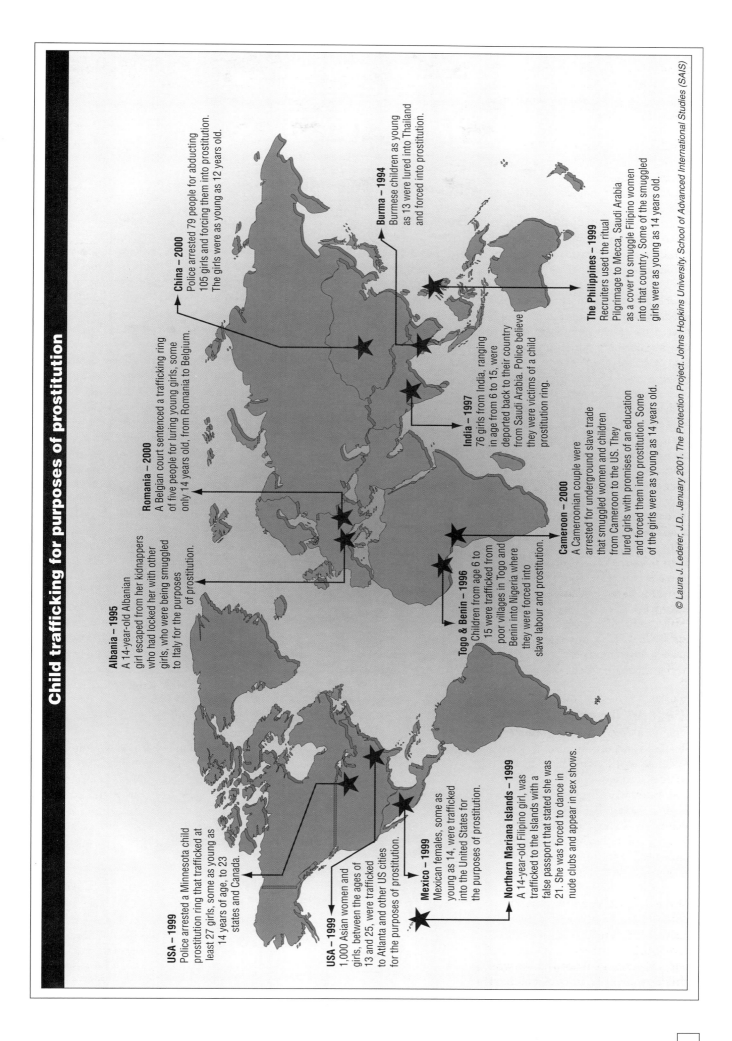

Albania – 1995
A 14-year-old Albanian girl escaped from her kidnappers who had locked her with other girls, who were being smuggled to Italy for the purposes of prostitution.

Romania – 2000
A Belgian court sentenced a trafficking ring of five people for luring young girls, some only 14 years old, from Romania to Belgium.

China – 2000
Police arrested 79 people for abducting 105 girls and forcing them into prostitution. The girls were as young as 12 years old.

Burma – 1994
Burmese children as young as 13 were lured into Thailand and forced into prostitution.

The Philippines – 1999
Recruiters used the ritual Pilgrimage to Mecca, Saudi Arabia as a cover to smuggle Filipino women into that country. Some of the smuggled girls were as young as 14 years old.

India – 1997
76 girls from India, ranging in age from 6 to 15, were deported back to their country from Saudi Arabia. Police believe they were victims of a child prostitution ring.

Cameroon – 2000
A Cameroonian couple were arrested for underground slave trade that smuggled women and children from Cameroon to the US. They lured girls with promises of an education and forced them into prostitution. Some of the girls were as young as 14 years old.

Togo & Benin – 1996
Children from age 6 to 15 were trafficked from poor villages in Togo and Benin into Nigeria where they were forced into slave labour and prostitution.

USA – 1999
Police arrested a Minnesota child prostitution ring that trafficked at least 27 girls, some as young as 14 years of age, to 23 states and Canada.

USA – 1999
1,000 Asian women and girls, between the ages of 13 and 25, were trafficked to Atlanta and other US cities for the purposes of prostitution.

Mexico – 1999
Mexican females, some as young as 14, were trafficked into the United States for the purposes of prostitution.

Northern Mariana Islands – 1999
A 14-year-old Filipino girl, was trafficked to the Islands with a false passport that stated she was 21. She was forced to dance in nude clubs and appear in sex shows.

Child soldiers

Information from UNICEF

Background

Over 300,000 children, at any given time are involved in military activity and armed conflicts throughout the world.

Many of these children have witnessed or taken part in terrifying acts of violence – even against their own families and communities. Child soldiers can be as young as seven or eight years old. Some armies abduct and coerce children into their ranks. Other children join because they have no option – often armies are the only places children can find shelter, food, and 'protection'.

The impact on children

Whatever the nature of their recruitment, children suffer profoundly from their involvement in military activity – an overwhelming abuse of their right to be protected from the effects of conflict.

Not only is their childhood destroyed, they are also separated from their homes, communities and families. Children's education is brought to a brutal end and military activity damages them physically and mentally.

Who are the child soldiers?

The term 'child soldiers' conjures up images of gun-toting adolescent boys, but a number of the world's child soldiers are girls and younger children. It is estimated that as many as one-third of all child soldiers in Ethiopia and Uganda are girls.

Children may also be involved in equally dangerous work as messengers, porters or cooks and girls are highly vulnerable to sexual abuse as the 'wives' of soldiers.

Small arms and light weapons

UNICEF believes that the widespread availability of small arms – some 500 million are currently in circulation – is having a direct impact on the numbers of children recruited into military activity. Many weapons are so light and portable that a ten-year-old can easily carry, strip and load them. A former child soldier in Northern Uganda highlights the problem:

'I learnt some things when I was with the rebels. I learnt how to shoot, how to lay anti-personnel mines and how to live on the run. I especially knew how to use an AK-47 twelve-inch, which I could dismantle in less than one minute.'

> **Not only is their childhood destroyed, they are also separated from their homes, communities and families**

UNICEF's response

UNICEF is actively involved in working to prevent the recruitment of children as soldiers. This ranges from global campaigning to encourage countries to make 18 the minimum age for the recruitment and deployment of soldiers, to negotiation and advocacy in individual countries. In Southern Sudan UNICEF has secured agreement from one of the main rebel forces – the Sudanese People's Liberation Army (SPLA) – that under-18s will no longer be targeted for recruitment.

Where children and young people have been involved in military activity, UNICEF supports centres to demobilise, rehabilitate and over time, reunite children with their families and reintegrate them into their communities. As a result of the damage inflicted on children such reintegration can be a very complex process.

In Uganda, children rescued from the Lord's Resistance Army are

helped to come to terms with their experiences through community-based counselling. They are able to renew their education, often through specially developed programmes for children who have missed many years of schooling and are trained in basic, practical skills such as tailoring or carpentry which will be of value to them, their families and communities.

Protecting children's rights
In September 2000 Prime Minister Tony Blair signed a new international agreement (known as an Optional Protocol to the UN Convention on the Rights of the Child) which obliges governments to take all feasible measures to end the deployment of under-18s as soldiers.

On signing the Optional Protocol, the government submitted a declaration reserving the right to deploy under-18s under certain conditions. By including this declaration UNICEF is concerned that the Government will continue to both recruit and deploy under-18s – contravening the spirit of the Optional Protocol, which was adopted to protect children from armed conflict.

Child soldiers and the UK
UNICEF is also concerned about child soldiers in countries which are not in active conflict. The UK for example actively targets under-18s to join its armed forces. Between 1998 and 1999, over 9,000 under-18s were recruited unto the armed forces. In addition, the UK is the only European country that routinely deploys under-18s into conflict zones. Under-18s fought in the Falklands and Gulf wars and four under-18s have been killed in combat since 1981.

A situation that can change
UNICEF firmly believes that under-18s should not participate in armed conflicts and should not therefore be recruited into armed forces or deployed into conflict situations.

UNICEF UK is lobbying the UK government to ratify the Optional Protocol without any reservations, and ultimately to stop recruiting and

deploying under-18s into the armed forces. UNICEF UK also works with other organisations on this issue as part of the UK Coalition to Stop the Use of Child Soldiers.

How you can help
UNICEF UK is working to encourage the government to ratify the Optional Protocol without any reservations. You can support the campaign and receive further information by:
- Contacting the UNICEF UK campaigns network. Please call

020 7405 5592 or e-mail campaigns@unicef.org.uk
- Visiting UNICEF UK's web site www.unicef.org.uk

Sources:
- *Growing up Alone: childhood under siege*, UNICEF UK May 2001
- *UNICEF actions on behalf of children affected by armed conflict*, UNICEF August 2000
- *United Kingdom Under 18s: Report on Recruitment and Deployment of Child Soldiers*, Amnesty International, November 2000

Useful web sites:
- UNICEF information on children in conflict www.unicef.org/children_conflict
- Coalition to Stop the Use of Child Soldiers www.child-soldiers.org

• The above information is from a UNICEF Information Sheet. See page 41 for their address details.
© UNICEF

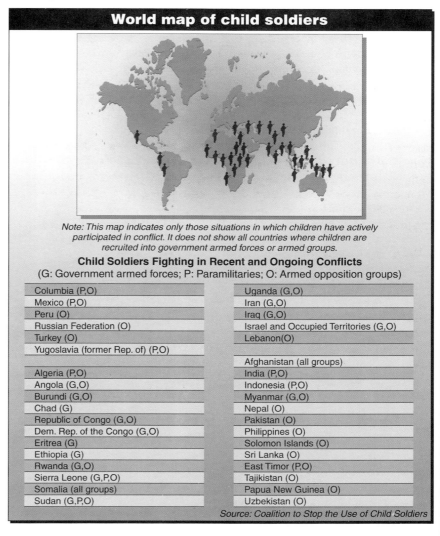

World map of child soldiers

Note: This map indicates only those situations in which children have actively participated in conflict. It does not show all countries where children are recruited into government armed forces or armed groups.

Child Soldiers Fighting in Recent and Ongoing Conflicts
(G: Government armed forces; P: Paramilitaries; O: Armed opposition groups)

Columbia (P,O)	Uganda (G,O)
Mexico (P,O)	Iran (G,O)
Peru (O)	Iraq (G,O)
Russian Federation (O)	Israel and Occupied Territories (G,O)
Turkey (O)	Lebanon(O)
Yugoslavia (former Rep. of) (P,O)	
	Afghanistan (all groups)
Algeria (P,O)	India (P,O)
Angola (G,O)	Indonesia (P,O)
Burundi (G,O)	Myanmar (G,O)
Chad (G)	Nepal (O)
Republic of Congo (G,O)	Pakistan (O)
Dem. Rep. of the Congo (G,O)	Philippines (O)
Eritrea (G)	Solomon Islands (O)
Ethiopia (G)	Sri Lanka (O)
Rwanda (G,O)	East Timor (P,O)
Sierra Leone (G,P,O)	Tajikistan (O)
Somalia (all groups)	Papua New Guinea (O)
Sudan (G,P,O)	Uzbekistan (O)

Source: Coalition to Stop the Use of Child Soldiers

A growing phenomenon

The use of children as soldiers. Information from the Coalition to Stop the Use of Child Soldiers

A number of factors have led to a steady increase in the use of children as soldiers. First, technological developments and the proliferation of weapons, especially small arms, have made semi-automatic rifles light enough to be used and simple enough to be stripped and reassembled by a child of 10.[1] A single pull of the trigger is enough to release a steady stream of bullets. Moreover, these weapons are not expensive. In some countries at war, an AK-47 may be bought for as little as US$20.

Second, the longer the conflict goes on, the more likely children are to be 'recruited', as the shortage of manpower, due to increasing casualties and escalation of the conflict, leads to an ever more desperate search for fresh recruits to fill the ranks. When they are not specifically sought out – for example, because they are perceived to make obedient soldiers – recruitment of underage children may occur because official procedures are not followed or because the children have no identity papers showing how old (or rather, how young) they are.

Some children volunteer to join up: in order to survive, to prove their manhood, egged on by peers or a culture of violence, or driven by a desire to avenge atrocities committed against their family or community. This is, however, a broad interpretation of the term 'volunteer', as brutal circumstance leaves little room for genuine choice. In the case of children who volunteered to join armed opposition forces in their respective countries, research conducted for the UN by the Quaker UN Office in Geneva showed that the single major factor of such volunteering is ill-treatment of themselves or their families by government troops.[2] Here, the lesson for governments engaging in internal repression is clear.

Although prevailing international law sets 15 as the minimum age for military recruitment and participation in armed conflict, there is widespread agreement that this age limit is too low and that it must be raised to 18. Although most countries prohibit recruitment and participation of under-18s, others have signalled their intention to continue to recruit 16- and/or 17-year-olds. The United States of America, for instance, the country most opposed to setting 18 as the minimum age for recruitment and participation,[3] recruits a tiny number of 17-year-olds – less than one-half of one per cent of its armed forces. However, tens of thousands of 17-year-olds technically become members of the armed forces each year in a programme that allows youth to delay beginning military training for weeks or even months.

The United Kingdom, which continues to recruit 16-year-olds on leaving school, actually encourages youth to start the recruitment process while still at school, leaving only the formal enlistment for later.[4] In a bid to swell the ranks of its armed forces, the UK recently embarked on a recruitment drive of under-18s. If a 16-year-old is enrolled – normally for 22 years of service – he or she has the right to 'buy out' after three years. The three-year period, however, only begins to elapse upon the recruit's 18th birthday – this is known as the 'five-year trap'.[5] British soldiers under the age of 18 fought – and died – in both the Falklands conflict and the Gulf War.

In addition to the UK and the US, other countries that recruit (i.e., conscript, enlist or otherwise accept into their armed forces) under-18s include Australia, Austria, Bangladesh, Bhutan, Bosnia-Herzegovina, Brazil, Burundi, Canada, Chile, Croatia, Cuba, Cyprus, Denmark, El Salvador, Estonia, Former Yugoslav Republic of Macedonia, France, Germany, Honduras, India, Indonesia, Iran, Iraq, Ireland, Israel, Italy, Japan,

Jordan, Laos, Libya, Luxembourg, Mauritania, Mexico, Namibia, Netherlands, New Zealand, Nicaragua, Norway, Pakistan, Peru, Poland, Qatar, Republic of Korea, Slovakia, Slovenia, Sudan, Uganda and Yugoslavia.[6] In a number of other countries, despite national legislation prohibiting the recruitment of under-18s, the use of children as soldiers has been recorded in both government armed forces and armed opposition groups.

Notes:
1   Report by Ms Graça Machel, Expert of the Secretary-General, on the Impact of Armed Conflict on Children, UN doc. A/51/306 of 26 August 1996, p. 14.
2   R. Brett and M. McCallin, *Children: The Invisible Soldiers*, p. 96.
3   The Defense Appropriations Authorization Act, passed by Congress and signed by the US President in October 1998, includes a provision specifically encouraging the US not to block 18 as the minimum age for participation in an Optional Protocol to the Convention on the Rights of the Child.
4   B. Hetherington, *Memorandum on the UK Government's policy on the* recruitment of young persons to the armed forces and on the engagement of young persons in armed conflict, Peace Pledge Union, UK, April 1998.
5   Ibid.
6   Information believed to be correct as at June 1999.

• The above information is an extract from the Coalition to Stop the Use of Child Soldiers' web site which can be found at www.child-soldiers.org Alternatively, see page 41 for their address details.

The voices of child soldiers

Information from Human Rights Watch

'The army was a nightmare. We suffered greatly from the cruel treatment we received. We were constantly beaten, mostly for no reason at all, just to keep us in a state of terror. I still have a scar on my lip and sharp pains in my stomach from being brutally kicked by the older soldiers. The food was scarce, and they made us walk with heavy loads, much too heavy for our small and malnourished bodies. They forced me to learn how to fight the enemy, in a war that I didn't understand why was being fought.'
Emilio, recruited by the Guatemalan army at age 14[1]

'One boy tried to escape [from the rebels], but he was caught . . . His hands were tied, and then they made us, the other new captives, kill him with a stick. I felt sick. I knew this boy from before. We were from the same village. I refused to kill him and they told me they would shoot me. They pointed a gun at me, so I had to do it. The boy was asking me, "Why are you doing this?" I said I had no choice. After we killed him, they made us smear his blood on our arms . . . They said we had to do this so we would not fear death and so we would not try to escape . . . I still dream about the boy from my village who I killed. I see him in my dreams, and he is talking to me and saying I killed him for nothing, and I am crying.'
Susan, 16, abducted by the Lord's Resistance Army in Uganda[2]

'They gave me pills that made me crazy. When the craziness got in my head, I beat people on their heads and hurt them until they bled. When the craziness got out of my head I felt guilty. If I remembered the person I went to them and apologised. If they did not accept my apology, I felt bad.'
a 13-year-old former child soldier from Liberia[3]

'I was in the front lines the whole time I was with the [opposition force]. I used to be assigned to plant mines in areas the enemy passed through. They used us for reconnaissance and other things like that because if you're a child the enemy doesn't notice you much; nor do the villagers.'
former child soldier from Burma/Myanmar[4]

'They beat all the people there, old and young, they killed them all, nearly 10 people . . . like dogs they killed them . . . I didn't kill anyone, but I saw them killing . . . the children who were with them killed too . . . with weapons . . . they made us drink the blood of people, we took blood from the dead into a bowl and they made us drink . . . then when they killed the people they made us eat their liver, their heart, which they took out and sliced and fried . . . And they made us little one eat.'
Peruvian woman, recruited by the Shining Path at age 11[5]

1   Testimony given at a Congressional briefing on child soldiers, sponsored by Human Rights Watch, Washington DC, 3 December 1997.
2   Human Rights Watch interview, Gulu, Uganda, May 1997.
3   Human Rights Watch interview, Liberia, April 1994.
4   Rachel Brett and Margaret McCallin, *Children: The Invisible Soldiers* (Radda Barnen, 1996), p. 127.
5   Center for Defense Information, 'The Invisible Soldiers: Child Combatants,' *The Defense Monitor*, July 1997.

• The above information is an extract from Human Rights Watch's web site which can be found at www.hrw.org Alternatively, see page 41 for their address details.

41 countries send children into war

By Peter Moszynski

Three hundred thousand children under-18 are participating in hostilities in some 41 countries affected by serious ongoing armed conflict, according to a new report from the Coalition to Stop the Use of Child Soldiers.

The report is highly critical of Britain – one of the few western countries to use minors in combat: 'The United Kingdom has persistently objected to raising the international minimum age for voluntary recruitment and participation in hostilities to 18.

'Within Europe the UK has the lowest minimum age for recruitment, the highest recruitment of under-18s into the regular armed forces and the lowest deployment age. The UK is also the only European country to send minors routinely into battle,' it says.

One of the worst affected countries is Sierra Leone, where thousands of children have been forcibly recruited into some of the most vicious fighting in the world today.

One former child soldier at a care centre in Lunghi run by the charity Caritas Makeni described how he had taken part in cross-border raids into Guinea. There they would surround villages and press-gang the youths into rebel forces – a method similar to that used by the Revolutionary United Front several years ago.

While hundreds of children have been demobilised in recent weeks, there is concern that many in Sierra Leone's civil defence force (CDF) will fail to be counted.

The disarmament process requires one weapon to be handed over for each person entering demobilisation. As each CDF detachment consists of about 30 people (about a third of them children) sharing around three weapons, care workers fear the numbers are severely under-reported.

Children serving in pro-government militias such as the Kamajors and Gbethis are mostly volunteers, unlike those abducted by the RUF. But Alphonso Bagni of Caritas said: 'Children serving in the CDF have often been as corrupted by the use of arms as those with rebel units.

> **'Within Europe the UK has the lowest minimum age for recruitment, the highest recruitment of under-18s into the regular armed forces and the lowest deployment age'**

'Ten-year-old kids fighting on the front line or demanding money while manning road-blocks often end up almost as badly socialised as the children abducted by their opponents.'

The danger of failing to demobilise pro-government militias was demonstrated by an incident last year involving the theoretically pro-government West Side Boys.

After the derailment of the peace process in May 2000, they began a campaign of pillage that culminated in the kidnap of British military advisers in August. In September British troops raided their hideout. The captives were freed but a rescuer was killed.

Olara Otunnu, UN special representative for children and armed conflict, says it is vital to give Africa's lost generation a stake in the peace: 'They have no choice but to deal with the children of war. They could be sitting on a time-bomb.'

Rory McGovern, of the Coalition, said: 'What happens in Sierra Leone will be a litmus test for efforts to stop child soldiering around the world. The international community knows what is needed – now we need to see the resources and political will to make it work.'

Due to the sensitivity surrounding the use of child soldiers in Sierra Leone, and the stipulation that no one under 18 is deployed in the new army being established by Britain's military training team (Matt), none of the army's estimated 5,000 17-year-olds are deployed there.

The UN recently forbade the use of under-18s in peacekeeping but British troops in the Nato-led K-For and S-For have no such restrictions.

Lisa Alfredson, a spokeswoman for the Coalition, said: 'It's ironic that Britain should itself recruit at the age of 16 and insist that the armies it is training should have a minimum recruitment age of 18.'

Although Britain has signed the optional protocol to the Convention on the Rights of the Child – the May 2000 amendment to the international law governing the rights of children which stipulates 18 as the minimum age for recruitment – it has exercised 'an interpretative declaration' on deployment.

Child soldiers

Information from Save the Children

Up to 300,000 children are fighting adults' wars around the world today. Save the Children believes this is wrong, and is trying to stop children being used in this way.

War is no place for a child. Yet children as young as seven are forced to become soldiers. Armies use children as soldiers in more than 30 countries today, including Angola, Colombia, Liberia, Sri Lanka, Sudan and Uganda. They are used both by 'regular' government forces and rebel armies.

Army chiefs like to recruit children because they are small, easy to intimidate, don't ask for wages, and are less likely to rebel or ask questions. They are also cheaper in other ways – they eat less food than big, adult soldiers. They can carry the lighter, modern weapons. Recruiters deliberately target children, and often make war sound glamorous to lure impressionable youngsters.

What makes children join up?

Many have no choice – they are rounded up and forced to fight. Others join because they are so poor. Often this is the only way to get food and clothes; they see joining an army as a way to survive. Most child soldiers come from very poor families, or from vulnerable groups like street children or refugees who may have no family around them. This makes them particularly vulnerable to being recruited. Some children have lost their families in war and want to get revenge for their deaths. Joining an army may give orphans a sense of belonging, almost like a replacement family.

Some children genuinely believe (or have been brainwashed into believing) that they're doing the right thing by joining a group of 'freedom fighters'. Having a gun, and giving orders, makes children feel powerful even if they're not. Children become soldiers for all these reasons.

Save the Children

How are children turned into soldiers?

They are often forced to do violent things to other people, so that they become hardened to violence. This is called becoming 'desensitised'. They may be beaten, drugged, and put through violent initiation rites. They are brainwashed into thinking they can't be harmed. Being forced to kill others – sometimes even their own friends and families – also makes children feel they have burned their bridges with the outside world. They dare not try to escape – not only for fear of being killed by the adult soldiers, but also because they fear being rejected by their communities. They feel they have done such terrible things, they can't go back – even though it wasn't their fault. This process is also deliberate; it's a way of forcing children to stay in armies.

Susan, 16, was kidnapped by rebels in Uganda. 'One boy tried to escape,' she says, 'but he was caught. Then they made us, the other new captives, kill him with a stick. I felt sick. I knew this boy . . . we were from the same village. I refused to kill him and they said they would shoot me. They pointed a gun at me, so I had to do it . . . Afterwards, they made us smear his blood on our arms. They said we had to do this so we would not fear death and so we would not try to escape . . . I still dream about that boy. I see him and he is talking to me and saying, "You killed me for nothing", and I am crying.'

What does this do to children?

It robs them of their childhood. They don't get the chance to go to school, or play, or be with their families – all the normal, everyday things that help children learn and grow. The whole experience wrecks children emotionally and physically. They may be killed, or injured for life. Their health is put at risk – they may be disabled, raped, or exposed to HIV/AIDS. Girls are often used sexually – they are kidnapped, raped, and forced to become the 'wives' of adult soldiers.

Children who have only known violence find it very difficult to become civilians again, and make normal relationships. Because they have missed out on school, they don't have the basic skills to hold down a job. Some of these children have never been to school and do not know how to read or write. They only know how to be soldiers. Their families may not want them back if they are mentally disturbed by their experiences, or because families fear they will bring shame on them.

What the law says

International laws allow children as young as 15 to fight. But the recruitment of child soldiers under 15 has been made a war crime, as a result of lobbying by Save the Children and other human rights organisations. Adults who recruit under-15s will be put on trial at the International Criminal Court. But it may take up to seven years for this court to start working.

The UN Convention on the Rights of the Child – the main international law which says what can and can't be done to children – bans governments from recruiting or using soldiers under 15. The UN has said governments must only send UN peacekeepers over the age of 18 on duties. Many governments also believe using child soldiers is a form of dangerous work and have tried and failed to pass international legislation on this. For example, Britain wants to continue to let 17-year-olds fight in its armed forces and has opposed new international legislation which would prevent the use of children under 18 being used as soldiers.

• Want to find out more about Save the Children and its work? If you have access to an Internet browser, visit the Save the Children web site: www.savethechildren.org.uk. You can also visit the Hot Savvy page and leave your thoughts.

A child labour issue

Child soldiers. Information from the Coalition to Stop the Use of Child Soldiers

Although some governments are still reluctant to acknowledge the fact, the use of children as soldiers should on many counts be considered as unlawful child labour because of the hazardous nature of the work involved. Indeed, research carried out for the UN Study on the Impact of Armed Conflict on Children shows that it is predominantly the same categories of children who are used as child soldiers in wartime as are drawn into exploitative forms of labour in peacetime.

The overwhelming majority of child soldiers come from the following groups:

- children separated from their families or with disrupted family backgrounds (e.g. orphans, unaccompanied children, children from single-parent families, or from families headed by children);
- economically and socially deprived children (the poor, both rural and urban, and those without access to education, vocational training, or a reasonable standard of living);
- other marginalised groups (e.g. street children, certain minorities, refugees and the internally displaced);
- children from the conflict zones themselves.

The International Labour Organisation (ILO) recognises that

'the idea of the minimum age for admission to employment or work which by its nature or the circumstances in which it is carried out is likely to jeopardise the health, safety or morals of young persons may be applied in corollary to the involvement in armed conflicts'.[1] Under ILO Convention No. 138 on Minimum Age, adopted in 1973, the minimum age for hazardous work is 18 years.

The new ILO Convention, adopted unanimously by the 174 Member States of the International Labour Organisation on 16 June 1999, commits each state which ratifies it to 'take immediate and effective measures to secure the prohibition and elimination of the worst forms of child labour as a matter of urgency'. The term 'child' applies to all persons under the age of 18 and the worst forms of child labour include 'all forms of slavery or practices similar to slavery, such as the sale and trafficking of children, debt bondage and serfdom and forced or compulsory labour, including forced or compulsory recruitment of children for use in armed conflict'.[2] This is the first time that an 18-year minimum age limit has been set in relation to child soldiering in an international convention. It is also the first specific, legal recognition of child soldiering as a form of child labour.

In addition, the Recommendation accompanying the new Convention sets out criteria to be considered in relation to the designation of hazardous work, implementing measures and a programme of action, including that: 'Members should provide that the worst forms of child labour are criminal offences . . . including forced or compulsory recruitment of children for use in armed conflict'.

Notes:
1 Comments on the report of the Working Group on a draft Optional Protocol to the Convention on the Rights of the Child on involvement of children in armed conflicts, contained in UN Doc. E/CN.4/ 1996/WG.13/2 of 23 November 1995, p. 12.
2 International Labour Office, Worst Forms of Child Labour Convention, 1999, Geneva.

Key findings on child soldiers

The Global Report on Child Soldiers analyses military recruitment by governments and armed groups in 180 countries

Trends of child soldiering

- More than 300,000 children are fighting with governments and armed groups in more than 40 countries around the world.
- In 87 countries children are recruited into government armed forces, paramilitaries, civil militia and non-state armed groups.
- 73 countries are known to uphold the principle that no one under the age of 18 be recruited militarily. The situation remains unclear in 25 countries.

Areas of progress

- In the last year, 80 countries have signed the Optional Protocol to the Convention on the Rights of the Child on the involvement of children in armed conflict, which sets 18 as the minimum age for direct participation in hostilities, for compulsory recruitment, and for any recruitment by non-governmental armed groups. Five have ratified (Canada, Bangladesh, Sri Lanka, Andorra and the Democratic Republic of Congo). The protocol is expected to go into force by the end of the year.
- Several governments have adopted new legislation raising the minimum age of recruitment to 18, including Colombia, Finland, Italy, Portugal and South Africa. Several non-governmental armed groups have also made commitments not to recruit children under the age of 18, for example the Restoration Council of the Shan State and the Shan State Army in Myanmar.
- The use of child soldiers in Latin America, the Middle East and the Balkans has decreased markedly as conflicts with high rates of child soldiering have come to an end. These include the civil wars in Central America, Lebanon, the Iraq-Iran war and the conflicts in the Balkans.
- Recent demobilisations of child soldiers have taken place in Sierra Leone (by the Revolutionary United Front) and Southern Sudan (by the Sudan People's Liberation Army).

Common issues

Widely perceived to be a cheap and expendable commodity, child soldiers tend to receive little or no training before being thrust into the front lines.

Children may begin participating in conflict from as young as seven years of age. Some serve as porters or messengers, others as spies. In Myanmar, for instance, children have been forced to sweep roads with tree branches or brooms to detect or detonate mines. As soon as children are strong enough to handle an assault rifle or semi-automatic weapon (normally at 10 years of age) they may be used in frontline roles.

Child soldiers are often treated brutally and punishments for mistakes or desertions are severe. In many countries, child soldiers who are captured, escape or surrender often face ill-treatment, torture or even death. In Colombia, the location of reintegration programmes is a closely guarded secret since child soldiers face severe security risks, including death.

Girls

Child soldiers are not just boys with guns: in many countries girls too are used as soldiers, though generally in smaller numbers than boys. In Sri Lanka, for instance, young Tamil girls, often orphans, have been systematically recruited by the opposition Liberation Tigers of Tamil Eelam (LTTE). Dubbed 'Birds of Freedom' many are reportedly trained as suicide bombers as they may better evade government security.

Girls are particularly at risk of rape, sexual slavery and abuse, although the exploitation of boys for these purposes is also reported.

Even in the supposedly sophisticated armed forces of industrialised countries, young recruits – especially girls – are subject to 'hazing', harassment and abuse. In the United States, one school district in Washington banned recruiters from schools after several Army recruiters from a local recruiting station were investigated for sexual harassment of high school girls. In recent years cases of bullying and humiliation of under-18 recruits in the British Army have included mock execution, forced simulation of sexual acts, 'regimental baths' in vomit and urine and the forced ingestion of mud.

Consequences

Besides the risk of death or injury in combat, child soldiers suffer disproportionately from the rigours of military life. Younger children collapse under heavy loads; malnutrition, respiratory and skin infections and other ailments are frequent. Child soldiers may also be at additional risk of drug and alcohol abuse (often used to recruit children or desensitise them to violence), sexually transmitted diseases, including HIV/AIDS, and unwanted pregnancies. Auditory and visual problems are common, along with landmine injuries.

Regional highlights

Sub-Saharan Africa

More than 120,000 children, some no more than 7 or 8 years of age, are currently fighting in armed conflicts across Africa: Angola, Burundi, Congo-Brazzaville, the Democratic Republic of Congo (DRC), Ethiopia, Liberia, Rwanda, Sierra Leone, Sudan and Uganda.

- Some children have been recruited from across their borders: in 2000, Namibian children were reportedly recruited by Angolan forces in the border region; Ugandan and Rwandan armed forces recruited children to militias they have backed in the DRC's civil war; Kenyan street-children have reportedly been recruited by Burundi Hutu militias active in the same conflict; Rwandan forces recruited children in neighbouring countries to fight in both the DRC and Burundi.

- In Sierra Leone more than 5,000 children served among government and opposition forces, a further 5,000 are estimated to have been recruited for labour among armed groups. In 2000 reports emerged of armed groups forcing children to work in diamond fields under their control. In recent weeks the RUF released more than 700 child soldiers as a result of peace talks, but child solders have been demobilised and re-recruited in the past.
- In Uganda, the LRA has systematically abducted over 10,000 children from their schools, communities and homes to camps in Sudan, forcing them to commit atrocities and become sexual slaves. Children who attempt to escape, resist, cannot keep up or become ill are killed.

Middle East and North Africa
In the past two decades the Middle East and North Africa have witnessed some of the worst and most egregious cases of the exploitation of children as soldiers. Today, while the situation is vastly improved, children under 18 across the region continue to serve with government and opposition armed forces or to be subject to various forms of militarisation in their communities and schools.

- Sudan has one of the worst child soldier problems in the world: children as young as 12 have been forcibly recruited into government-aligned and separatist groups in the south of the country. The Government of Sudan has also provided support and protection to the Lord's Resistance Army (see above), responsible for the abduction, brutal treatment and sexual

slavery of over 10,000 Ugandan children.

- In Iraq, thousands of children aged 10 to 15 participate in the Ashbal Saddam (Saddam Lion Cubs) and receive training in the use of small arms, hand-to-hand combat and infantry tactics.
- Various Kurdish armed groups in northern Iraq, Iran and Turkey have reportedly used children as young as ten. Opposition groups in Algeria and tribal groups in Yemen have also used child soldiers.

Americas
Although the incidence of child soldiering has reduced and conflicts receded across the region, in some countries children continue to fight in internal conflicts or be forcibly recruited into government armed forces. The countries most affected by this problem have been Colombia and Peru, although large numbers of children are serving in the Paraguayan armed forces and problems are reported in Mexico.

- Over 14,000 Colombian children have been fighting with guerrilla groups and paramilitaries.
- In Paraguay, 56 under-18s died during their compulsory military service, six of them under the age of 18 in 2000 alone.
- The US has acknowledged that 17-year-old soldiers served in US military operations in the Gulf War, Somalia and Bosnia.

Asia and the Pacific
The worst affected countries in the region have been Afghanistan, Myanmar, Sri Lanka and, in the recent past, Cambodia.

- The Taliban that controls much of Afghanistan's territory continues to recruit young men trained and indoctrinated in Islamic schools, or madrasas, in

---

Sudan has one of the worst child soldier problems in the world: children as young as 12 have been forcibly recruited

---

neighbouring Pakistan. The Northern Alliance is also reported to have stepped up recruitment of children as its military situation deteriorates.

- Myanmar has one of the highest numbers of child soldiers in the world, both within governmental armed forces and non-governmental armed groups.
- The Liberation Tigers of Tamil Eelam (LTTE) of Sri Lanka has thousands of children serving in its ranks, despite repeated commitments not to recruit below 17.
- Children have joined political and sectarian militias in Indonesia and are fighting in Aceh, Papua and Kalimantan.

Europe, Russia and Central Asia
Children have participated in several European conflicts in recent years, mostly with armed opposition groups but sometimes with government-aligned paramilitaries. Children have spied, conveyed messages, carried weapons and ammunition, and, inevitably, killed and been killed in Bosnia-Herzegovina, Chechnya, Nagorno-Karabakh, south-east Turkey, Kosovo and Macedonia.

- In the last couple of weeks, an Albanian rebel commander stated to journalists that the National Liberation Army is using children against government forces in Macedonia.
- There are disturbing reports about the attachment of young orphans and street children as young as nine to military units and camps in Russia.
- The United Kingdom is the only European country to routinely send 17-year-olds into combat, even though they are not allowed under national legislation to drink, vote in elections or even join the police force.
- More than half of all Organisation for Security Cooperation in Europe (OSCE) member States accept under-18s into their armed forces.

• The above information is an extract from *Global Report on Child Soldiers 2001*, produced by Human Rights Watch. Visit their web site at www.hrw.org or see page 41 for their postal address details.

© 2001, Human Rights Watch

Children swap murder for maths

Colombia's government has set up safe houses with the aim of rehabilitating former rebel soldiers as young as 12

Marisol, 16, appears to be an ordinary schoolgirl. She dislikes maths, her spelling is not always perfect, and she says that when she finishes school she would like to be a pop singer.

Six months ago, however, Marisol was a commander in Colombia's largest rebel army, leading a column of 100 guerrillas in a string of attacks against army bases and police patrols.

'I was a good fighter and a good commander, but I had no freedom. All I had was war,' she said.

Marisol talks confidently about weaponry and tactics, but she now faces what may be her toughest battle so far: returning to civilian life after five years on the front lines of Colombia's bitter civil war.

An estimated 6,000 children fight with the rebels and rightwing paramilitaries, and as more children are sucked into the conflict, the Colombian government has opened a network of halfway houses to help fighters like Marisol who desert or are captured by the army.

Aged between 12 and 17, most of the young ex-combatants have experienced fighting, and all face enormous difficulties after leaving the war.

'When all you can expect is death, you have no vision of any future. We try to help the kids to think ahead, and realise that they can decide what will happen in their lives,' said Julian Aguirre, who runs the rehabilitation programme for the Colombian Family Welfare Institute.

The Revolutionary Armed Forces of Colombia (Farc) is the largest recruiter of children. The oldest rebel faction, it had just 1,000 guerrillas 20 years ago, but now fields 17,000 fighters, owing in part to the widespread use of child soldiers.

'In some regions recruitment is

By Martin Hodgson in Bogota

indiscriminate. I've heard Farc commanders saying that they'll take anyone big enough to hold a rifle,' said Mr Aguirre.

About one-quarter of child combatants are press-ganged, but the majority are volunteers. Some – like

> **'When all you can expect is death, you have no vision of any future. We try to help the kids to think ahead, and realise that they can decide what will happen in their lives'**

Marisol, whose father was a Farc commander – have family ties with the rebels; others join up to flee domestic violence or sexual abuse. But most go to war for want of any other options.

According to Rocio Mojica of Save the Children, 3m of the country's 14m children have no access to education. In much of rural Colombia, there has never been a consistent state presence or investment in education and the local economy.

'There are very few opportunities for work or education, and joining an armed group gives young people a sense of importance and belonging that they can't find elsewhere,' she said.

Miguel scraped just three years of school, and at 15 he was working as a bus driver's assistant when rightwing paramilitaries offered him a job.

They paid him £300 a month – more than three times the minimum wage – and equipped him with a pistol, a radio and a mobile phone. At first, his duties were minimal: he carried messages and patrolled the hills around his home town in central Colombia. But two months after joining up, he was ordered to torture and kill a suspected guerrilla.

'The "paras" said that if I didn't kill him, they'd shoot me because I knew too much,' Miguel said. After the murder, the paramilitary commander forced him to drink the victim's blood.

'Once you've done that three or four times you don't respect anything. You just kill for the sake of killing.' Miguel fled the group in July. He now lives at the same shelter as Marisol.

Plagued with nightmares, he initially found it hard to trust his former enemies. Now, his best friends are ex-guerrillas, but he still dreams nearly every night of the man he tortured to death.

'The ghosts inside are very strong. Most of the kids suffer from anxiety and depression,' said Carmen Liliana Forero, a teacher at the centre.

The past can reach out in more deadly ways. Guerrillas and para-militaries share the grim policy of murdering both deserters and former enemies, and the shelter's location is kept a closely guarded secret.

In a secluded country home, 20 children undergo psychological help and receive a basic education as well as various vocational skills.

'The idea is to help them become productive, so that when they leave the centre, they neither return to the war nor turn to crime,' Mr Aguirre said.

The children usually remain at the home for an average of four to six months while they decide what to do next. Those who can, return home. Others are sent to foster parents.

'Many of these kids will never see their families again,' said Mr Aguirre.

Mileidy, 18, is one of the lucky ones. It is her last day in the shelter before returning to the family she has not seen for five years. She joined the Farc because her parents couldn't afford school fees, but now she wants to become a social worker. She grins nervously at the thought of civilian life.

'It's going to be hard to start over with my family, but you can get used to anything. I don't know what will happen, but at least I know that I'm out of the war,' she said.

The use of children as soldiers

Information from the Coalition to Stop the Use of Child Soldiers

'I would like you to give a message. Please do your best to tell the world what is happening to us, the children. So that other children don't have to pass through this violence.'

The 15-year-old girl who ended an interview to Amnesty International with this plea was forcibly abducted at night from her home . . . by the Lord's Resistance Army (LRA), an armed opposition movement fighting the Ugandan Government. She was made to kill a boy who tried to escape. She witnessed another boy being hacked to death for not raising the alarm when a friend ran away. She was beaten when she dropped a water container and ran for cover under gunfire. She received 35 days of military training and was sent to fight . . . the government army.[1] More than 300,000 children under 18 are fighting in armed conflicts in more than thirty countries worldwide.

Hundred of thousands more children have been recruited, both into governmental armed forces and armed opposition groups.

While most child soldiers are aged between 15 and 18, many are recruited from the age of 10 and sometimes even younger.

In many countries, both girls and boys are used as soldiers; girls are at particular risk of rape, sexual harassment and abuse.

The widespread availability of modern lightweight weapons enables children to become efficient killers in combat; child soldiers are often used for special tasks, including to commit atrocities against their own families and communities.

While many children fight in the front line, others are used as spies, messengers, sentries, porters, servants and even sexual slaves; children are often used to lay and clear landmines.

The problem is most critical in Africa and Asia, though children are used as soldiers by governments and armed groups in many countries in the Americas, Europe and Middle East.

While some children are recruited forcibly, others are driven into armed forces by poverty, alienation and discrimination. Many children join armed groups because of their own experience of abuse at the hands of state authorities.

Both governments and armed groups use children because they are easier to condition into fearless killing and unthinking obedience; sometimes, children are supplied drugs and alcohol.

Children are often treated brutally and punishments for mistakes or desertion are severe; children are injured and sometimes killed during harsh training regimes.

The longer conflicts continue, the more likely children will be subjected to this abuse.

Towards a ban on child soldiers

There is a growing international consensus against the use of children as soldiers:

- The new International Criminal Court will treat the use of child soldiers as a war crime
- The International Labour Organisation (ILO) has defined child soldiering as one of the worst forms of child labour
- The UN Security Council, the UN General Assembly, the UN Commission on Human Rights, the Organisation for African Unity, the Organisation of American States and the Organisation for Security and Cooperation in Europe have all condemned this abuse

International humanitarian law and the UN Convention on the Rights of the Child set 15 as the minimum age for military recruitment and participation in armed conflict. But a new Optional Protocol to the Convention on the Rights of the Child

- prohibits governments and armed groups from using children under the age of 18 in conflict;
- bans all compulsory recruitment of under-18s;

- bans voluntary recruitment of under-18s by armed groups;
- raises the minimum age and requires strict safeguards for voluntary recruitment

More and more governments around the world are raising the age of recruitment to their armed forces to the 18 standard. The UN Secretary General has set 18 as a minimum age for UN peacekeepers. Even some armed groups, seeking recognition and legitimacy within the international community, have acknowledged the principle.

The use of children as weapons of war is like the use of landmines or chemical and biological weapons – simply unacceptable in any circumstances.

Note
1   Amnesty International: *Uganda: 'Breaking God's commands' : the destruction of childhood by the Lord's Resistance Army. 18 September 1997, AI Index: AFR 59/01/97.*

• The above information is an extract from the Coalition to Stop the Use of Child Soldiers' web site which can be found at www.child-soldiers.org Alternatively, see page 41 for their address details.

© Coalition to Stop the Use of Child Soldiers

Stop the use of child soldiers!

Information from Human Rights Watch

'I've seen people get their hands cut off, a ten-year-old girl raped and then die, and so many men and women burned alive . . . So many times I just cried inside my heart because I didn't dare cry out loud.'
Fourteen-year-old girl, abducted in January 1999 by the Revolutionary United Front, a rebel group in Sierra Leone

In dozens of countries around the world, children have become direct participants in war. Denied a childhood and often subjected to horrific violence, some 300,000 children are serving as soldiers in current armed conflicts. These young combatants participate in all aspects of contemporary warfare. They wield AK-47s and M-16s on the front lines of combat, serve as human mine detectors, participate in suicide missions, carry supplies, and act as spies, messengers or lookouts.

Physically vulnerable and easily intimidated, children typically make obedient soldiers. Many are abducted or recruited by force, and often compelled to follow orders under threat of death. Others join armed groups out of desperation. As society breaks down during conflict, leaving children no access to school, driving them from their homes, or separating them from family members, many children perceive armed groups as their best chance for survival. Others seek escape from poverty or join military forces to avenge family members who have been killed.

Child soldiers are being used in more than thirty countries around the world. Human Rights Watch has interviewed child soldiers from countries including Angola, Colombia, Lebanon, Liberia, Sierra Leone, Sudan and Uganda. In Sierra Leone, thousands of children abducted by rebel forces witnessed and participated in horrible atrocities against civilians, including beheadings, amputations, rape, and burning people alive. Children forced to take part in atrocities were often given drugs to overcome their fear or reluctance to fight.

In Colombia, tens of thousands of children have been used as soldiers by all sides to the country's ongoing bloody conflict. Government-backed paramilitaries recruit children as young as eight, while guerrilla forces use children to collect intelligence, make and deploy mines, and serve as advance troops in ambush attacks.

In southern Lebanon, boys as young as twelve years of age have been subject to forced conscription

Frequently denied an education or the opportunity to learn civilian job skills, many find it difficult to re-join peaceful society

by the South Lebanon Army (SLA), an Israeli auxiliary militia. When men and boys refuse to serve, flee the region to avoid conscription, or desert the SLA forces, their entire families may be expelled from the occupied zone.

Girls are also used as soldiers in many parts of the world. In addition to combat duties, girls are subject to sexual abuse and may be taken as 'wives' by rebel leaders in Angola, Sierra Leone and Uganda. In Northern Uganda, Human Rights Watch interviewed girls who had been impregnated by rebel commanders, and then forced to strap their babies on their backs and take up arms against Ugandan security forces.

Because of their immaturity and lack of experience, child soldiers suffer higher casualties than their adult counterparts. Even after the conflict is over, they may be left physically disabled or psychologically traumatised. Frequently denied an education or the opportunity to learn civilian job skills, many find it difficult to re-join peaceful society. Schooled only in war, former child soldiers are often drawn into crime or become easy prey for future recruitment.

• The above information is an extract from Human Rights Watch's web site which can be found at www.hrw.org Alternatively see page 41 for their postal address details.
© 2001, Human Rights Watch

World treaty set to ban children in combat

A ban on the use of children as soldiers, a human rights violation suffered by nearly half a million minors worldwide, has been approved by nearly a hundred countries in a treaty on the issue that entered into force 12 February 2002.

The juridical instrument, known as the Optional Protocol to the Convention on the Rights of the Child on the Involvement of Children in Armed Conflict, establishes that no one under 18 shall be compulsorily drafted into military service.

The Protocol also requires that governments raise the minimum age for voluntary enlistment in military institutions to 16.

The United Nations High Commissioner for Human Rights, Mary Robinson, said her office is 'urging all governments and armed groups to end the military recruitment of children under 18 and to release and rehabilitate those children already in service'. 'There can no longer be any excuses for using children for war,' Robinson added.

A half-million minors serve in governmental, paramilitary and other sorts of armed forces in 85 countries around the world, says the non-governmental Coalition to Stop the Use of Child Soldiers.

Of that half-million, more than 300,000 participate in active combat in armed conflicts under way in more than 35 countries, according to the Coalition, founded in 1998 to mobilise international public opinion against the use of minors in war.

The participation of children in wars is comparable to the use of landmines or chemical or biological weapons: unacceptable under any circumstances, said Rory Mungoven, director of the coalition.

The Optional Protocol, adopted in May 2000, has been signed so far by 94 countries. Just 14 have ratified the treaty. The document enters into force after the first 10 ratifications.

Mungoven criticised the slowness of the Protocol ratification process. The Coalition leader stressed that governments and armed groups that utilise children among their ranks must be rebuffed in the international arena.

> **The UNHCR is urging all governments and armed groups to end the military recruitment of children under 18 and to release and rehabilitate those children already in service**

The most egregious cases of child recruitment are found in Africa and Asia, though it also occurs in the Americas, Europe, and Middle East.

Most of the minors enlisted as soldiers worldwide are 15 to 18 years old, but in many cases children as young as 10 are recruited, and at times they are even younger. Girls as well as boys are used as soldiers. However, girls are at particular risk of rape, sexual harassment and abuse.

There has been some progress in the recent years with some governments and guerrilla organisations announcing the demobilisation of minors.

The countries that have ratified the Protocol on child soldiers are Andorra, Bangladesh, Canada, Czech Republic, Democratic Republic of the Congo, Iceland, Kenya, Monaco, New Zealand, Panama, Romania, Sri Lanka, the Vatican and Vietnam.

The entry into force of the Optional Protocol on the Involvement of Children in Armed Conflict is the second recent victory in favour of the consolidation of children's rights. On 18 January 2002, another Protocol to the Convention on the Rights of the Child took effect, banning the sale of children, child prostitution and child pornography, aimed at protecting an estimated one million children who are victims of this sort of exploitation around the world.

© Global March Against Child Labour

ADDITIONAL RESOURCES

You might like to contact the following organisations for further information. Due to the increasing cost of postage, many organisations cannot respond to enquiries unless they receive a stamped, addressed envelope.

Anti-Slavery International
Thomas Clarkson House
The Stableyard, Broomgrove Road
London, SW9 9TL
Tel: 020 7501 8920
Fax: 020 7738 4110
E-mail: info@antislavery.org
Web site: Web site:
www.antislavery.org
Anti-Slavery International is the world's oldest international human rights organisation, founded in 1839. Works at local, national and international levels to eliminate the system of slavery around the world.

Christian Aid
35 Lower Marsh
Waterloo , London, SE1 7RT
Tel: 020 7620 4444
Fax: 020 7620 0719
E-mail: info@christian-aid.org
Web site: www.christian-aid.org.uk
Christian Aid works in over 60 countries helping people, regardless of religion or race, to improve their own lives and tackle the causes of poverty and injustice.

Coalition to Stop the Use of Child Soldiers
PO Box 22696
London, N4 3ZJ
Tel: 020 7226 0606
Fax: 020 7226 0208
E-mail: info@child-soldiers.org
Web site: www.child-soldiers.org
An international movement of organisations and individuals committed to ending the use of children as soldiers.

Global March Against Child Labour
L-6 Kalkaji
New Delhi 110019I, India
Tel: + 91 11 622 4899
Fax: + 91 11 623 6818
E-mail: childhood@globalmarch.org
Web site: www.globalmarch.org
The Global March Against Child Labour is an international movement dedicated to giving every child a chance to live and grow without the burden of exploitative work.

ECPAT UK
Thomas Clarkson House
The Stableyard, Broomgrove Road
London, SW9 9TL
Tel: 020 7501 8927
Fax: 020 7738 4110
ecpatuk@antislavery.org
Web site: www.ecpat.org.uk
ECPAT stands for End Child Prostitution, Child Pornography And the Trafficking of children for sexual purposes. ECPAT UK campaigns for British legislation to be amended so that it protects all children, both in the UK and overseas, from commercial sexual abuse.

Human Rights Watch
33 Islington High Street
London, N1 9LH
Tel: 020 7713 1995
Fax: 020 7713 1800
E-mail: hrwuk@hrw.org
Web site: www.hrw.org
Human Rights Watch conducts regular, systematic investigations of human rights abuses in some 70 countries around the world. Human Rights Watch addresses the human rights practices of governments of all political stripes, of all geopolitical alignments, and of all ethnic and religious persuasions.

Save the Children
17 Grove Lane, Camberwell
London, SE5 8RD
Tel: 020 7703 58400
Fax: 020 7703 2278
Web sites:
www.savethechildren.org.uk
www.savethechildren.org.uk/rightonline
www.savethechildren.org.uk/education
Save the Children is the leading UK charity working to create a better world for children.

United Kingdom Committee for UNICEF
Africa House, 64-78 Kingsway
London, WC2B 6NB
Tel: 020 7405 5592
Fax: 020 7405 2332
E-mail: info@unicef.org.uk
Web site: www.unicef.org.uk
UNICEF, the United Nations Children's Fund, is a global champion for children's rights which makes a lasting difference by working with communities and influencing governments.

The World Bank
1818 H Street, N.W.
Washington, D.C. 20433, USA
Tel: + 1 202 477 1234
Fax: + 1 202 477 6391
Web site: www.worldbank.org
The World Bank Group works in more than 100 developing economies with the primary focus of helping the poorest people and the poorest countries.

World Vision UK
World Vision House
599 Avebury Boulevard
Milton Keynes, MK9 3PG
Tel: 01908 841000
Fax: 01908 841021
E-mail: info@worldvision.org.uk
Web site: www.worldvision.org.uk
World Vision works to provide the people of the United Kingdom with the most effective ways to help the world's poor build a better future for themselves and their children.

41

ACKNOWLEDGEMENTS

The publisher is grateful for permission to reproduce the following material.

While every care has been taken to trace and acknowledge copyright, the publisher tenders its apology for any accidental infringement or where copyright has proved untraceable. The publisher would be pleased to come to a suitable arrangement in any such case with the rightful owner.

Chapter One: Child Labour

Child labour, © Anti-Slavery International, *Child labour: the situation*, © Source Unattributable, *No cinderella story*, © Global March Against Child Labour, *The invisible girl*, © The World Bank, *China's children labour round the clock*, © Guardian Newspapers Limited 2001, *Child labour*, © Human Rights Watch, *Worst forms of child labour*, © Global March Against Child Labour, *Slave trade or fair trade?*, © Anti-Slavery International, *The bitter taste of chocolate*, © AFRICANEWS 2001, '*Chocolate slaves' carry many scars*, © Telegraph Group Limited, London 2001, *Warning over child slave trade*, © Guardian Newspapers Limited 2001, *Child labour in the shadow of the World Cup*, © Global March Against Child Labour, *Solutions to child labour*, © World Vision, *Child labour*, © World Vision.

Chapter Two: Sexual Exploitation

Commercial sexual exploitation, © UNICEF United Nations Children's Fund, *Sexual exploitation*, © Source Unattributable, *Sexual abuse and exploitation*, © Human Rights Watch, *Sexual exploitation of children*, © ECPAT UK (End Child Prostitution, Child Pornography And the Trafficking of children for sexual purposes), *Sex trafficking of children still not a crime*, © Christian Aid, *British sex tourists*, © World Vision, *Debunking the myths*, © UNICEF United Nations Children's Fund, *Child trafficking for purposes of prostitution*, © The Protection Project, Johns Hopkins University, School of Advanced International Studies (SAIS).

Chapter Three: Child Soldiers

Child soldiers, © UNICEF United Nations Children's Fund, *World map of child soldiers*, © Coalition to Stop the Use of Child Soldiers, *A growing phenomenon*, © Coalition to Stop the Use of Child Soldiers, *The voices of child soldiers*, © Human Rights Watch, *41 countries send children into war*, © Guardian Newspapers Limited 2001, *Child soldiers*, © Save the Children, *A child labour issue*, © Coalition to Stop the Use of Child Soldiers, *Key findings on child soldiers*, © Human Rights Watch, *Children swap murder for maths*, © Guardian Newspapers Limited 2001, *The use of children as soldiers*, © Coalition to Stop the Use of Child Soldiers, *Stop the use of child soldiers!*, © Human Rights Watch, *World treaty set to ban children in combat*, © Global March Against Child Labour.

Photographs and illustrations:

Pages 1, 12, 26, 30: Pumpkin House, pages 3, 24, 33: Fiona Katauskas, pages 5, 15, 20: Bev Aisbett, pages 8, 14, 19, 25, 28, 37, 40: Simon Kneebone.

Craig Donnellan
Cambridge
April, 2002